How To Run a Preschool Dance Studio

The 7 step system to create,
grow and expand your
preschool dance classes

Emma Franklin Bell

This book is dedicated to all the dance teachers, who want to take their studios, their students and themselves to the next level of success in dance.

Contents

Acknowledgements   vii

Preface   ix

Foundation Chapter   xi

CHAPTER 1
Branding   1

CHAPTER 2
Marketing   15

CHAPTER 3
The Dance Program   47

CHAPTER 4
Teachers and Training   65

CHAPTER 5
Customer Relationships and
Communication Skills   109

CHAPTER 6
Pricing, Payment and Profit   133

CHAPTER 7
The Business Systems   147

Final Thoughts   171

About the Author   177

ACKNOWLEDGEMENTS

MY THANKS GO TO THE MANY TEACHERS WHO SAW MY POTENTIAL and gave me the opportunity to expand my creative horizons through dance. Namely the teachers who had the most impact on me were Kim Walton, Tanya Pearson OAM, Marie Walton-Mahon, Sheila Laing and John Byrne. I would also like to offer thanks and acknowledgement to Louise Taylor, the first teacher who gave me an opportunity to teach in her school, this was where my eyes opened to the wonderful world of teaching and choreography.

The joy and the challenge of dance that only dancers truly understand has allowed for some incredible life long friendships namely Alexandra Lopez, Hugh Sheridan, Alexis Guest, and Stephanie Crowley - dear friends who've trained alongside me in many a studio and at many a barre. I also owe thanks to my Aunt Diana Carroll and Cousin Claire who took me in as a boarder at 16 years old when I pursued performing arts in Adelaide. To Clint Salter, a dear friend who also has as much passion for this industry as I do and is a wonderful entrepreneur, creative talent, marketer and loyal and inspirational friend. I owe thanks to my wonderful friend Anya Aytemiz and her gorgeous daughter Scarlett Brassington who was featured in all the early newspaper editorials and articles, without these early images we wouldn't have captured the essence of the Fairy Footsteps story from the beginning. I also send out thanks to my loyal dear friend Sarah Turier Evans who has always been supportive of my endeavors.

I'd like to acknowledge Kelliann Brady and Hayley Boardman for accepting the challenge to become the first teachers in my own preschool dance studio. These two fantastic women rose to the challenge and accepted the task of teaching in a studio with a completely different business model which meant they were literally 'going it alone' as I was not living in the same state as they were. I really am grateful for their commitment, capability and enthusiasm.

I'd like to acknowledge my wonderful dear Mum for driving me to ballet lessons five - six days a week and to both Mum and Dad who believed talent should be fostered and potential should be realized, without them I wouldn't have had the great career in dance I've had. Lastly, I'd like to thank dance – what dance gives you, what it teaches you about yourself and who you become in the process. Your dance training and your dance teachers never leave you, they are the elusive backdrop that shape the whole way you turn up in life, it shapes your approach, your presentation, your discipline and your creativity.

PREFACE

CONGRATULATIONS FOR DECIDING TO BUY THIS BOOK AND HAVING a desire to take the action steps to achieving the success you want in your preschool dance studio!

In the following modules I have put everything on the table for you, I really open up about everything I did, created and developed. I share with you all the elements I used and what made my preschool dance studio work so well so quickly.

A bit of background...

After 11 years in small business and 20 years in the dance industry I took a chance in 2012 and decided to write my own preschool ballet program, Fairy Footsteps. I created, set up and built a ballet school from scratch. Within 3 months the school had a second location and a second teacher with more classes expanding as time went on. We were featured in the media and had over 300 students go through the program in the first 18 months.

I was running the administrative side of the business from Sydney, NSW where I lived while the dance school operated in Perth, WA. I had an abundance of raving testimonials, no outstanding fees and no complaints. Mid 2014

I decided to sell the ballet studio to pursue other opportunities. The ballet studio still continues to grow and has expanded to further locations.

People started to ask me how I managed to run the studio the way that I did, so I started to write a newsletter around business and life based on what I'd learnt. If you're interested to sign up you can at www.emmafranklinbell.com. Before long I distilled what I had done down to seven steps, which became the book you have in your hands – How to Run a Preschool Dance Studio.

To be perfectly upfront and honest, just like a wonderful restaurant, a fantastic show or a five-star hotel there is never one magic thing that makes these experiences successful. There's not a magic pill, silver bullet or quick fix. For something to beautifully and seamlessly work, it's a combination, a cocktail if you like of a number of key things that make it work. So you wont be finding the answer in a few hints and tips or wacky tricks, it really takes all 7 steps.

These 7 modules cover the thought, the process and the sophistication needed to create, grow and expand into a school that works for you and allows you to run a business that's got passion, profit and purpose! This book is also now a successful program delivered as a 1-to-1 course of private mentoring sessions.

To Your Success,

Emma Franklin Bell

FOUNDATION CHAPTER

IT'S IMPORTANT TO START ANYTHING IN LIFE FROM A REALLY solid foundation. If we launch in with both feet and we don't really know why we're doing something, sometimes later down the track we can find ourselves in a bit of a rut wondering why we started.

There are 7 key things that need to be touched on before we jump in to something new. We really have to come to the understanding that any new project is going to ask of us more than facts and figures but also a strong and wise mindset. I have identified that these 7 key areas need to be touched on before we dive in to the mechanics of running a studio. Being aware of these things will start us off in good stead so we can then pump up the volume and turn our business ideas into reality!

The 7 Foundational Keys:
1. Responsibility
2. Acceptance
3. Why
4. Values
5. Vision
6. Commitment
7. Action

Your Responsibility

It is essential for us to come to a point in our lives where we realize – if it's going to be, it's up to me!

When I was in my 20s I thought that somehow "magically" it would all just "work out" I don't really know how I came up with this idea. I thought the man would just come along – he didn't. I thought the magic job would arrive – it didn't. I thought University would have the answers – it didn't. I wound up at 28 thinking "Geez, the only way to really get moving, make something happen and get going is to take 100% responsibility for my current situation and quite simply – start making it happen!"

The moment we take ownership of our situation and our skills is the moment we are liberated. Taking 100% responsibility for our lives shifts us out of any sort of victim role, pushes the inner persecutor in us away and allows us to rise above drama and become true leaders on our own personal march towards our dreams!

Your Acceptance

In life, as we know, there are many, many things out of our control. There are also no guarantees in life except for death, taxes and change – everything else is unpredictable. Once we are able to accept life and circumstances for what they are, (even though we may not always agree with the situation), we can learn to accept it, take ownership and decide the best course of action. Relinquishing the need and the urgency to control everything around us is a much more peaceful and relaxed state. This relaxed state is what we need to aim for when we live in a world of expectation, rush, demand and stimulation. Take the time out to accept what you have now, where you're going and what your plans are. As the saying goes 'work with what you have, where you are now' and in time you will move closer to where you want to go.

Your Why

Taking the time out sometimes to remember 'why' we started our dance studio or why we want to start a dance studio/business in the first place is really important. Not only for our sanity but to reignite our passion!

Remembering our early days, our achievements and our journey allows us to see we've come a long way and done an awesome job! It also helps us soldier on when things can become challenging. Here are 3 simple questions to get us thinking about our 'Why':

Write down your answers to these questions. Writing helps ideas and thoughts to sink into our brain and we are more likely to remember them and think about them and act on them.

1. Take me back – Why did you start dancing? How did it make you feel?
2. In the beginning - What was it that led you to want to start your own school/studio?
3. The Art of Dance - What is it about dance and teaching that you're passionate about?

Your Values

One of the most important things in our lives is to know exactly what we value. Our values guide us to where we want to go in our lives. Sometimes we can wind up feeling fed up, confused or frustrated and often it's because we haven't stayed in alignment with our values.

Values are deep and important to us on a personal level. They may be things relating to health, friends, partner, excellence and so on. Whatever they are, I encourage you to write down 4 important key things/areas that you value in your life. It's good to rewrite them every year.

Here's an example:

I value my strong, healthy body and looking after my health and wellbeing

I value my 5 longest, oldest friendships

Write down your 4 most important values here.

MY CORE VALUES

1.

2.

3.

4.

It's important to read our values everyday to remind ourselves that we are sticking to what we believe in.

Your Vision

As the Bible said: 'Without vision the people will perish.' Without your own sense of where your dance studio is going and what you want to achieve you may end up somewhere you'd rather not be. A vision needs to be a few clear, strong goals that you work towards.

Vision Questions

Remember: Write down your answers...

- If you imagine you are running your school in three years time, how does it look?
- How many students do you have?
- What's the main focus of the school? Dance style and student type?
- Are you in other locations?
- How many teachers do you have?
- What is your school known for?
- As a teacher/studio director what are you known for?
- How much revenue is the school doing?
- How much net profit are you making?
- What's your personal weekly salary? Has this increased in three years?

Your Commitment

You are the only one that can take you from where you are today reading this book to where you want to be in the future. Every decision and choice you make at any moment will impact your outcome. Making a solid commitment to read, think, listen and take action on things that you believe are effective is crucial to your overall success. I encourage you to sit up, open up and get ready to absorb and commit to the learning in front of you.

Your Action

After people commit, it is most important that they follow this up by taking action. Taking action is way easier said than done, there are lots of things that stop us, restrict us and immobilize us from taking action. Before we know it, we haven't done it.

We've stopped and not followed through on what we said we would and yet the most powerful thing at the end of the day is taking action. If people hadn't taken action we wouldn't have the motorcar, the airplane, the mobile phone. If people thought about how cool the idea was but then didn't act on the idea humanity wouldn't move ahead.

People who take action, get up, get the resources, take the training, make the phone calls, write the plan, meet up with that person, and then continue to take action. They never stop. They are do-ers!

Action is the most important thing that we can do, because it means we actually DO IT!

Don't be stopped by someone; don't listen to people who tell you, you can't do it. (Maybe don't tell everyone your ideas – keep them as secrets and slowly but surely work away at them, only tell a few people that you trust!)

Most people who have gone on to do great things have been told, "It won't work" "You'll never make it" "Nobody will read that" "You'll lose money" and so on.

You need to rise above that and take action today.

Clarity Moving Forward

It's really crucial to take the time out to do these exercises in this foundation module and to really think about the 7 key areas that have been touched on. These things really will have you gain great clarity about who you are, why you're doing this, where you want to go and how you want to show up in the world.

I strongly encourage you to think deeply about these core aspects of yourself moving forward and keep them in mind when you're working through the 'practical' sides of the dance studio.

CHAPTER 1

BRANDING

BRANDING IS SO IMPORTANT FOR DANCE STUDIO OWNERS THESE days. With new dance studios springing up all the time, we really have to keep our brands strong. This means everything from our website, our logo, our customer service, our teaching, our teachers, our uniforms, our ideals and our mission.

Tight branding is going to make you unique and remembered; it will also position you in the market place and develop your reputation.

What is a brand?

Think about Apple, BMW, Target, Gucci, and Virgin. When you think about these brands, thoughts come to mind; in your head you might think 'cool and trendy', 'rich and suave', 'cheap but well made', 'fun and adventurous.' All these thoughts that come to mind are from what's called in the marketing and advertising world 'branding'.

A brand is what generates the thoughts, feelings and attitudes about or toward something. So rather than thinking about the features like 'white and flat screen' or 'good brakes and leather interior,' instead you are thinking about the feelings and the attitudes you get about the company as a whole.

Branding is used as a means to send a message out to you. Branding messages can be sent to you via the following.

- Quality of products
- Price but also 'value' of the product
- Customer service
- Culture – does it seem young and funky, conservative or outdated?
- Verbal messages – what taglines, dialogue are used in advertisements?
- Celebrity endorsements – who is the 'face' of the product?
- Reputation – word of mouth
- Trust relationship with that brand often based on past experience

There are a number of factors that make you feel something towards a brand. A main part of branding is what you can't see.

Your aim is to stand out, stand strong and get noticed. Gone are the days of doing a letterbox drop and hoping people will enroll. You want your classes and school to be noticed, known and remembered. This will bring you students, opportunities and financial reward - great things that we all need and want in order to run a successful dance school.

Branding is easy and fun. Don't get caught up worrying that you may not be any good at it or you don't really know what do to. It's one of those things you can quickly and easily pick up and develop.

Your Business Name

The name you have chosen or you are in the process of choosing for your school will be everywhere from your Facebook page to your return address labels. Here are some key things to be mindful of when choosing or changing your business name:

Choose a name that people can say and remember easily. Do they get tongue-tied pronouncing your business name? Is it a made up name? Is it in another language? This can cause confusion. Make sure the name is clear, crisp and simple and that anyone from your next-door neighbor's 10 year old through to her Grandma can say it and remember it. Mums would tell me that their children would say "Am I going to Fairy Footsteps today?" Children as young as 3 years old were able to say the name and understand it, which was fantastic for us because they knew our name and were remembering the brand.

Business name registration - depending on where you are located make sure you've checked out that you can be the owner of the business name you've chosen. In Australia, ASIC is the government agency that is in charge of registering all business names. Check this first, before getting the domain name for your website.

Domain name availability - you may have the perfect business name chosen but has someone got the domain name already? Ensure the domain name is available and that no one is doing something similar with a similar name.

Colors - think about the group you're targeting which is mainly Mums and sometimes Dads or grandparents of preschoolers and the preschoolers themselves. You want to tap into the childlike, emotional and creative aspect of what you're offering. Brainstorm colors that you like that are also aligned with the group you're dealing with. Are you connecting with them? You need to appeal and connect to the children as well as the parents.

Logo Artwork - I would absolutely highly recommend a logo of some sort. We humans are so visual that sometimes it's probably the logo more than the name that people will remember. The logo needs to conjure up a feeling and response in people that makes them think about children, dance, imagination, movement, joy, fun and so on.

A Brand is what a brand does

We've touched on the technical stuff around thinking up and registering names and also the visual side of the colors and logo designs but a brand is also what a brand does.

What does this mean?

Over the next few modules you'll learn everything from marketing to metrics and the reason why the brand module is first is that I want you to be reading through everything else with your brand in mind. Below I outline what I mean by 'a brand is what a brand does.'

A brand is the following:

The *feeling* your business has in the eyes of your customer.

The way you, the business owner, shows up - How do you present? How do you speak to students and parents? What do you say? What do you not say? What are your emails like? What's the tone of the voice in emails?

Your website and marketing - What's the quality of your website and your brochures? Are you professional? Premium? Homely? Community? Your brand ripples right through everything.

Your pricing - Are you cheap and cheerful? Are you premium? Do you stand by your brand with conviction and make sure you get paid on time?

Your teachers are your brand ambassadors - Your teachers are a direct reflection of your brand. Are your teachers young and fun? Older and more serious? What vibe are your teachers sending out?

Your dance program - Do you make it up week by week? Do you prepare lessons? Or do you follow an already created and crafted program? How you deliver your classes and the level of sophistication reflects directly on your brand.

Customer service - this one is probably the biggest of all. The way you interact with your customers, everything from that first phone call to recital or concert day and everything in between is a reflection of you and your brand and even one slip up can affect your reputation.

BRAND DEVELOPMENT FOR YOUR STUDIO – CORE BUSINESS

Developing a strong, known and liked brand is about taking the time to sit down with a coffee and think about: 'What would I like to be *known* for in my chosen field of dance?'

Answering this question with integrity, truth and clarity will help you develop the depth behind everything you do and this really is what ripples through the brand that people come to know.

It is important to start to decide what core style you want to be known for. Ballet? Hip Hop? Triple-Threat? This then has you more focused when you speak to people, post images, write up plans for the future and so on.

BRAND QUIZ

Ask yourself the following questions and write down your answers:

1. What do I really love about dance?
2. What do I really love about children?
3. What 3 words would I use to describe myself?
4. What 3 words would I use to describe my studio or the studio I'm starting?

This quick quiz gives you an idea of how you feel inside yourself about dance, children and your vision. These answers are allowing us to dig a little deeper into the emotional part of ourselves and this helps develop your brand from not only how it looks but also how you want to present and be seen in the community.

My Personal Story When Developing the Fairy Footsteps Brand

When I sat down and decided to create my own pre-school ballet school I was really clear on the brand. I wanted the whole 'feeling' to be imaginative, whimsical, balletic, fairy-themed, magical and creative. I made sure that every key piece of the business reflected this. These are the areas of the school I worked on to create that brand 'feeling'.

- Logo
- Name
- Images
- Colors
- Uniform
- Props
- The way we interacted with parents
- Newsletter
- Teachers' outfits and attitude
- Facebook updates
- Teachers' handbook
- Music

STUDENT UNIFORM BRANDING

Fuchsia Pink Tutu Story

When I was running my preschool dance business I wanted the class uniform to be a strong branding element. I chose fuchsia pink tutus that matched my logo colors. This enhanced the brand because parents knew that little girls in the fuchsia pink tutus went to Fairy Footsteps. Other pre-school ballet classes I observed dressed their girls in light pink, although absolutely lovely, this meant that to a degree you couldn't really differentiate the schools. At the time, no one else was wearing fuchsia pink.

People underestimate something as simple as the uniform however it is one of the most vital branding elements. It's what the children wear every week, it's what stands out in all the photos plus it creates a 'feeling' for not only the little girls but the school as a whole.

I also made it very clear that it was absolutely essential that every child wore the tutu to class every week, it was provided as a non-negotiable part of the fees and so became an expectation. I would explain to parents that the 'ritual' of learning what's expected of you when you go to a ballet class is really important and that it had an impact on the personal pride of the students.

Even though some of the children were as young as 2½ they were given the due respect that ballet is sophisticated and with that comes self-discipline. Therefore all children were expected to wear their tutu and their leather ballet shoes. No one rebutted this policy because it was set and was not let slip.

BRANDED CLASSES

Each class and style should be branded, meaning it has a great name for the program plus it has its own logo. You might run a jazz class for under 5s call it something funky like 'Glitter Jazz', 'Jazz Stars' or for a ballet class it could be called 'Rainbow Ballerinas' or 'Flower Fairy Ballet'. Branded programs generate more professionalism and can ask for a more premium price. Have the name, the brand, the feel and the culture in mind when you are creating your program. (Module 3 we work on the program).

PERSONAL BRANDING/IMPRESSION MANAGEMENT - BRAND YOU

You are the spokesperson, the advocate, the ambassador and the PR person all rolled into one. The way **you are** has a huge impact on your dance school's success because you are the head honcho - the go-to person for your business.

How can you be awesome at Brand You?

Here are some key how-tos:
- Always return phone calls within 24 hours
- Always answer emails within 24 hours
- Always have a genuine smile
- Always dress well to show that you take yourself, your school and your students seriously. Your students deserve nothing less.
- Never gossip to anyone about students or parents, set high standards of behavior
- Have your personal Facebook and other social media profiles set to the highest level of privacy setting so that random people can't snoop at your personal photos or status updates.
- Always be on time.
- Talk about meaningful things that paint the best and most truthful impression of you.
- Never bring your emotions, down days or problems into the studio.

- Always show respect - you need to set the standard of behavior for your studio even if others don't always do the same.
- Never lower your standards.
- Create boundaries between yourself and your relationships with parents, staff and other key people (more on this in the customer relationships module).

All the above will add up to you presenting yourself as a calm, professional, respectful, dignified person who can be trusted and taken seriously.

There are three main areas to think about in terms of understanding more about you and your personal brand:

1. Your personality and character
2. Your uniqueness and distinctiveness
3. Your values and beliefs

These three elements are extremely personal and they are all about clearly defining you as an exciting, authentic and unique person! Then the next part of your personal brand experience is about getting out there, getting ahead and getting noticed!

These are the types of messages you send out by just being you:

1. Quality of your skills, ideas and standards
2. Customer service – how you treat people
3. Culture – do you seem young and funky, conservative or friendly?
4. Verbal messages – what language do you use? Are you articulate?
5. Your reputation – word of mouth from others

6. The 'trust' relationship with you.How do people feel about you from past experience?

Just by existing and being a person you are sending out messages to the world and those around you and as the director of a studio it is really important to know how you are being perceived. This aspect of branding is what's called a 'Personal Brand.'

Very successful people understand that developing and defining their personal brand will be an enormous advantage to the success of their career.

To start to discover our own individual personal brand answer these few questions, based on the points above.

1. If you had to rate the 'quality' of your work in your own business and if outstanding quality was 10, mediocre was 5 and low was 1 what would it be?
2. How do you treat everyone you meet and everyone you're involved with in work and personal life?
3. Choose 3 words to describe what sort of cultural feel or vibe you give out?
4. How do you speak? What style of language do you use? How do you sound to others?
5. If you overheard someone talking about you and your studio, what would they be saying?
6. Do people feel they can trust you? Do you follow through on arrangements? Do you complete projects with people? Are you honest and reliable?

PERSONAL BRAND PROMOTIONAL OPPORTUNITIES

If you are interested in promoting yourself in the dance community or the small business community, consider how you may be able to do this. This is not for everybody but some people do see the value in enhancing their own personal profile in order to be more involved in the community and also to promote their studio.

If this interests you, consider the following:

- Which media could you be featured in?
- What presentations could you give and where?
- What events could you host?
- Which columns/blogs could you write or contribute to?
- Which networking events could you attend in your local area?

SOCIAL MEDIA PLAN

Write a detailed overview of how active you are on each social media portal.

Answer these questions for each portal e.g. Facebook, LinkedIn and Twitter:

- How often do you post?
- Are there lots of friendly photographs of you and the school?
- Do you link your e-newsletter to your social media page?
- How many people are in the group/liking your page/ following you?
- Regarding blogs – do you write your own? Do you comment on other dance blogs?

- Regarding dance websites – do you notice who is active and what they're doing? Do you write articles or conduct interviews that can then go on that dance website with a link back to your studio's website?

Now create a list of all the websites you visit that are related to dance. These may be Australian or overseas websites, some of them may also be Facebook pages or Twitter pages. Think about how often you go on these websites and what sections you read most. There may be an opportunity for you to contribute or cross promote in some way.

In Summary...

- **Branding is the feeling people get about you and your studio when they see your logo/name/website and other branded collateral.**
- **A brand is what a brand does**
- **Choose a name that sticks, that people can say and understand**
- **Ripple your branding right through everything from the emails to uniforms**
- **Develop and enhance your personal brand**

CHAPTER 2

MARKETING

MARKETING IS ONE OF THE MOST IMPORTANT ASPECTS OF YOUR studio's success. Without marketing, people do not know about you and if nobody knows about you then no customers will come along. Marketing is the lifeblood of your business it is what drives sales.

Effective marketing is all the activity, strategy, promotion and advertising that you do that works as a funnel to drive people to you and then you have the potential to convert them into happy, paying parents.

Marketing is no Magic Bullet

Each dance school is very different therefore there is no magic bullet that can be given to everyone that will result in making your school the talk of the town. Effective marketing that I discuss over the next few pages is based on what I used, what I've used with clients and also the principles and ideas that form the basis of solid, effective marketing.

Marketing is a massive subject area and encompasses many aspects but to kick off, marketing must be consistent. If it's something you use every now and then it is a promotion, not marketing.

Marketing is a consistent, long-term strategy that leads to new students. It isn't flash in the pan or quick fix.

Marketing No-Nos!

Don't:

- Only market when you need new students (this is a promotion not marketing)
- Only market at the beginning of terms
- Think marketing is mainly publicity
- Think marketing is sales
- Market to everyone who dances
- Focus on the latest things your school is offering
- Forget to calculate the cost of your marketing vs. your results (return)

Marketing Must Dos!

Do:

- Market your school all the time – all through the year
- Use Social Media almost everyday
- Know what your core business is
- Market yourself as the studio owner

- Market your school in line with timely topics in the community
- Have a marketing budget for the year
- Have a strong brand
- Get known for a key part of the dance studio (something you do in your school that's strong that can be drawn out and focused on)
- Build partnerships

Marketing is a well-rounded approach to amplifying you, your studio and what you offer. It must be something that is thought out, planned, timed and stuck to.

Your Marketing Budget

It's really important that one of the first things you do around marketing is sit down and nut out your budget. Realistically, at the end of the day, how much do you have to spend? Look at the amount you have to spend for the whole year. Then divide that by 12 and you have your marketing budget per month. This allows you to be marketing in a variety of ways every month.

If you haven't planned out the facts and figures on your budget, you may spend way over your capacity which will damage your business or if you don't organize enough marketing you may end up losing out because you haven't generated enough paying customers.

3 Types of Customers:
1. New: Acquisition - getting new customers
2. Current: Retention - keeping current customers
3. Past: Winning Back - reaching out to past customers

Customer building through marketing can include:

- Trial Classes
- Newsletters
- Website
- Facebook adverts
- Newspaper adverts/editorials
- Fetes and festivals
- Paying to be on another person's newsletter
- Kid's directories
- Dance shops - flyers, timetable, shout-out on Facebook
- Free Tutus
- Referral program

Trial Classes

Initially when you are opening up in a new suburb you may want to hold a few free trial classes. This is recommended to get noticed and get known when you are new.

Hold free trial classes on exactly the same day, same time and same venue where you will be holding the actual classes at normal class times. If you hold them at a different day/time/venue and then you try and feed people across to your actual classes people get confused.

After you've been established for 6 months or more and your student numbers are good, only hold 'trial' classes not 'free' trial classes. This is much more effective for your bottom line. In essence a 'trial' class means that if someone comes to a trial class then enrolls for the full term they pay for that initial 'trial' class too.

If they don't enroll then they just participate in that trial class and they leave. It is basically an 'obligation-free' trial not a 'free trial'. This has been highly successful in my experience.

You can hold these trial classes right throughout the term till about week 4 or 5. It's worth cutting off any new students entering class from week 5 as the preparation for Demonstration Day (explained in module 3) gets into full swing and it's too difficult for new students to integrate into the group and learn the work late into the term.

Newsletters

(Are for retaining and winning back customers)

The email newsletter is a very important feature of your overall marketing strategy. It makes you stay 'top of mind'. Top of mind is the notion that when people think of a particular industry, they think of you. By having an e-newsletter pop into their inbox every 3-4 weeks you are 'reminding' people that you are around, still operating and still offering great classes.

1. It's advised to send out a newsletter about once per month or more, updating parents on all relevant news past and upcoming
2. Aim for the second week of the month
3. Schedule it to be sent at 8am, Monday morning
4. Use Mailchimp (up to 2000 people on your list are free) or some other free newsletter service.

When I was running my dance school I would send a newsletter out at the following times:

One week before term starts - the subject line would be 'Back to Ballet Next Week' - this always got replies as some people often just needed to be reminded, as they are very busy.

Week 4 of term - if it was a 9 or 10 week term (the usual) I would send a newsletter one month in. People are then settled into the term and you can inform them of any news, remind them of term dates and recital, concerts or demonstration days.

Four weeks in also means that if some people missed the beginning of term enrolment they may want to do a mid-term enrolment, which can be mentioned in the newsletter and is a great way to boost numbers in classes that may be a bit thin.

Week 8 of term - this newsletter is a reminder that 'Demonstration Day' or an end of term recital or concert is coming up in two weeks. You can talk about how fantastic the term has been these last two months and how much the students are learning.

You can also include key dates - end of term date, demonstration day date and next term enrolment details and dates. By all means feel free in this email to talk about and remind them about the next term's enrolments.

Items to include in the body of your dance school e-newsletter:

- Your logo at the top

- **Your contact details** - social media and website links
- **Opening paragraph** - this is from you, it opens the newsletter (a bit like an editor in a magazine). You say any friendly, personal or important things and also what is included in this current newsletter. Always sign off with your name and you may include your teachers' names as well.
- **'Key Dates' or 'Dates for your Diary'** - include any important dates next so this is right upfront in the reader's mind.
- **Image** - next you need an image of some kind to break up the text or people won't read it. This can be a photo of some of the children in class, a photo of some ballet or dance news that's current or a photo of a current touring show.
- **Dance shop** - include the details of the local dance shop. I find one of the key questions I would always get asked would be about where to buy dancewear, shoes etc. If the details are in the newsletter that's a quick and easy way to let everyone know.
- **Dance image and quote** - end the newsletter with a dance/ballet image (preferably of children) with an uplifting quote on it. Go to Google or Pinterest and search for images with quotes. Always include the source i.e. 'Photo courtesy of...' and just be aware of copyright issues when choosing your image. If you're unsure about using an image email the person or company who owns it and ask for permission.
- **Sign off** personally at the bottom of the newsletter.

Other things you can include throughout the year in your newsletter:

A competition - this makes people interact with you and it is also friendly and fun. You can make the competition open to 'current members only' or everyone on your database list. Prizes can include: DVDs, tutus, movie tickets, free lessons, a ballet pack with say a book and a few gifts with ballet images on them.

Advertising someone else's business - you may have been approached or you approach people and say for $20 or $50, whatever you decide, that you will advertise their business in your newsletter. There needs to be an offer for your readers. Make sure the business is aligned somehow with dance, children, children's services or activities, education, Mums and Dads, the local area etc. The ad has to be something that would appeal to the people who read your newsletter.

Ballet news - If there are key things happening in dance include them in your newsletter so that your subscribers are getting informed about the industry and you show that you are up to date.

Student of the month - some dance schools will feature a 'Ballerina of the Month'; have a photo of them and a little Q & A. This can be fun and creates a nice community feel in the dance studio. You could also do a Q & A with a teacher, costume maker or any other staff member.

Recipes - you can include healthy recipes for parents that feature foods that are nutritious but also give children energy.

Your own advertising - you can include adverts for Free Trial classes, tutus, shoes or any other things you sell. This reminds people of all the things you sell. You may also include an offer or discount on one of your products.

Tell us in 25 words or less - you can run a competition where the prize is a ballet pack (e.g. tutu, book, a bag etc and it needs to be quite substantial so that people bother entering :) You would say 'Tell us in 25 words or less what you love about...' (insert your dance school name here) or 'Tell us in 25 words or less what we could do to improve our school' or 'Tell us in 25 words or less something outstanding about one of our teachers'. This allows you to gain info and valuable feedback from your customers.

You can then use these as testimonials (with permission of course) and market research. Only a small percentage will usually reply, that's OK, any inside info is valuable and worth the effort to get.

On the Website

Your website may not be the first place someone lands as these days it is commonplace for people to go straight to a Facebook page first. However, your website will be visited at some stage in the buying cycle to check out your location, timetable, teachers and fees. Your website ideally needs to have the following:

- **Presentation** – Avoid using white writing on a black background, keep written content to a minimum, have a lot of photos of you, the students and the studio.

- **Phone number** - Have your phone number in the top right hand corner, or somewhere prominent on the front page.

- **Video** – If possible have a video that introduces you and the school with snippets from your students, teachers and shots of the studios.

- **Sign Up** – Have a sign up box of some sort on the home page. This might be for a trial class, a free gift, a competition or an instant download. Whatever it is, have it on the homepage with an easy-to-fill-in sign-up box with just name and email fields. This way, you're not only building your list but you can email the person back and start a conversation around what they'd be interested in regarding your classes.

- **Content** – The writing on the website needs to be all about 'them' meaning all about the parents and the children. Talk about the nurturing environment of the studio, building children's confidence and all the opportunities the children get to enjoy when becoming a part of your studio. The 'vibe' of the studio needs to come through the written content and it needs to invoke emotions and make the reader 'feel' something positive in relation to your school as soon as they read it.

- **Testimonials** – Ideally it is wonderful to have testimonials on the homepage and around the website in general. This makes parents feel comfortable to send their child to your school and it backs up their argument for choosing your school over another one.

- **Strong Logo/Brand** – This needs to be front and center, not lost in the bowels of the website. You need to be projecting your logo loud and clear on every page. Ideally, keep the logo at the top of every page.

- **Pages** – Make sure you include:
  - Homepage – Featuring the above points.
  - About Us – Story, Teachers, Founder.
  - Classes & Fees – Locations, Fees, Uniform, Terms & Conditions.
  - Gallery – You might have photos from classes and concerts.
  - Media – Articles, Videos, Interviews.
  - Contact Us – All contact details, email submit form and social media icons.

Other pages to consider:
- Trial Class – A page that has the trial class form on it for parents to easily fill out.
- Shop – To sell your branded merchandise or dance accessories.
- Blog – This can be a copy of your newsletter posted on your website or dance news or general updates you want to keep people updated on.
- Program – Explain aspects of your dance program, have photos or videos available.

Facebook Adverts

In the early days you really want to build up your 'likes' on your Facebook business page so you have a solid audience to speak to. You need to encourage everyone in the dance school to like your Facebook page.

How to do this:

- Have the Facebook 'like' link or button at the bottom of all your emails in the signature tag
- Have your friends and family 'like' the page, this is effective for the page reach regarding their contacts and friends seeing your page
- Say to people when you are talking to them "please head to the Facebook page and like it as that's where I keep everyone informed and up to date".
- Have the Facebook icon at the top of all the news-letters
- Have the Facebook icon very visible on every page of your website
- Ask teachers to actively get likes

Once you've got everyone liking the Facebook page you can then increase your likes by promoting your page. Go to the section that says 'Get more likes' or in the 'Ads Manager' section and find the 'Increasing likes' function.

'Like' tips:

Ensure you target the location for the likes - find the box that allows you to select the suburbs that you want to target (near your dance school).

Make sure you set the date. Don't let Facebook just have your campaign going on and on. Very important - **set the dates for your campaign.**

My tip: Only run the campaign for 2 days at a time. I'd aim for between Tuesday and Thursday however different groups of people are different. You may find that weekend is good for your people. Play around with different 2 days slots until you find which one is the most successful.

I'd only look at spending $20-30 each time you run a campaign. Likes seem to generally work out about $1 each (don't quote me) so it's up to you how much you want to spend.

The ideal is to have friends of friends liking and then the organic, natural increase in likes starts to happen. This will increase once more people know about you. In the early days you want to generate and populate your Facebook page to increase exposure and be able to be more viral when you post and one way to do this is to use adverts initially to boost your likes.

Don't be tempted to 'buy' likes from places like Fiverr or other places that may offer this service, as fake likes are not honest, not useful and not effective.

Boosting Posts:

When you do a post that you think is great for showcasing your dance school be sure to 'boost' it. **Things to note:**

Facebook is sneaky and doesn't show **all** your posts to **all** your fans **all** of the time. No doubt because then you wouldn't boost your posts.

When you boost your post it gets seen by lots more people, so make sure that what you're boosting is interesting and enticing so the maximum number of people read it.

When boosting be sure to do a range of boosting: to your list of likes, their friends and also to new people who haven't liked your page yet but are in the suburbs you want to target. Then list all the suburbs you want to target to see your post (similar to what you did in the likes campaign).

I've found that the most effective response seems to come from doing an offer like 'come along to a trial class - fill in the form here' (insert a link in the post to your form). Be sure to include photos of students in your posts when you can, as photos are very popular for generating interest and attracting new customers.

Facebook doesn't like to boost things that look like adverts and they will 'disapprove' boosts that look like ads and then your boosted post won't run. Generally this is usually assessed on the amount of writing that is on the image included in the post. So, make sure you mainly use photos with no writing on them and do the writing in the text box where you update the status. You can even add a link in the comments box.

People also say that if you put more than one photo, (say three or four) in your updates they are seen by more people. If you have multiple photos, upload them in one bunch so people can flick through them all.

Facebook changes a lot, you have to keep up with the trends of what the latest is regarding what's working and not working when it comes to Facebook posting, advertising and engagement. I suggest following Amy Porterfield or Rick Mulready to stay updated.

Instagram

A fair few dance studios are using instagram and taking photos of classes, the studio, themselves, behind the scenes etc. Some people have found this to be helpful and useful for attracting new customers. Some teachers have also informed me that when parents take photos and put them on instagram this can be effective for generating new customers and interest. I would look closely at the photographic privacy laws before becoming too involved in an open forum like instagram or twitter.

Newspaper Adverts
(To gain new customers)

When starting this new section of your school or starting your dance studio from scratch you want to really get the word out there to your community. Find out about all the local papers in your area, ring them all and find out the costs for an ad of the same size so that you can compare prices. Also ask if they do any deals e.g. if you take out 3 ads (1 per week x 3 weeks) is that cheaper than a one-off?

With some papers if you run a slightly bigger, more expensive ad you also get a free editorial sometimes with a photo included.

Newspaper Advert Tips to Increase Success:

Always do the following:

- Have your brand name at the top so people can see it and recognize it instantly
- Have an image or photo to evoke emotion
- List only the necessary details: phone number, website address and locations
- Do an offer: a free trial class, free tutu, free face painting
- Have the ad in color
- Don't have too much writing on the ad - keep words to the absolute minimum

I found that running Free Trial class offers were more effective and viable for our school than offering a free tutu but everything is worth trying out. Just make sure that you always check the results of your ads - how many phone calls, emails did you get? How many people came to your Free Trial class? How many actual new students did you get as a result of the ad? Ask people if they saw your newspaper advert.

You then measure these results against the cost of the ad and work out if it was cost effective. Newspaper ads are expensive so be sure to check that they are paying off in terms of children coming to trial classes or enrolling directly from parents seeing the ad.

Editorials

Editorials (an article about you and your school) are so important for your marketing and a lot of people read them. A photo evokes emotion and makes people feel more familiar with you and your school.

Tips for writing your own newspaper editorial:

- Come up with a fun, catchy headline
- Keep it short - 120-150 words
- Talk about something that's happening (this is 'the angle') and not just your school, e.g.
  - New classes opening
  - Free Trial classes
  - Open day with Free Face-painting
  - New location or studio
  - Charity event
  - Sponsoring something
- Get a quote from a parent and put it in the editorial (include their name and get their permission)
- Say who, where, when and what the story is about in the first five sentences
- Include a short quote from you in the story
- Say what the classes involve that you are writing about (what the kids do and what they get out of it)
- Put your name, phone number and website at the end of the story if the paper will let you

After a while the press gets to know you and certain journalists may take an interest in you if you're doing things for the community, running events, introducing a new dance style and so on. We found that the press came to us within a year because we had become quite well known and had built good relationships with the press. We then managed to get a fantastic big article with lovely full color photos in the Mandurah Mail newspaper without paying a cent.

Fetes/Festivals/Charity Events (To gain new customers)

Over the years I've been involved in a range of community events. I've performed at fetes and festivals, I've been on the committee or team organizing community festivals and been involved with election campaigns and run activities at charity events.

These types of events are good for your overall marketing and goodwill - they are not the be all and end all of getting known but they do allow you to be seen and to be genuinely involved in your local community of which your dance school is an important part.

Finding Events

One way is to scour all the local news and websites and contact the local council for upcoming events in the suburbs where you have classes. Find out when they are on, who the contact person is and what your options are.

Key questions to ask the organizers about having a stall at an event:

- How many people are expected to attend each day?
- How many stalls will there be?
- What's the stall size and layout and the different costs for different stall sizes?
- What is included in hiring a stall or space? Do you get an umbrella? A cover? Tables? Chairs?

- What happens if it rains?
- Included in the stall fee are there any other offers such as getting advertising in the newsletter or on the website of the organization hosting the event?
- What insurance do I need and what is the cost?

You can also ask about the options for being a **sponsor** of the event instead or as well as being a stallholder, then ask:

- How much is it to be a sponsor for the event?
- What are the packages they offer?
- Where will my logo be displayed?
- Where and when will my brochures, pens, gifts etc be handed out or are they included in show bags?
- Do I get a mention/logo in the events newsletter, brochure, on the website or Facebook page?
- Are there any other similar or competing businesses also sponsoring?
- Can I have a pull-up banner or A-frame displayed somewhere at the event?

Don't be timid about asking these questions - this is about presenting in a 'business like' way when discussing these types of options. Once you have found out the answers to all your questions for any upcoming events that are suitable, you then want to weigh up the following things:

- Does it cost more or less to have a stall or be a sponsor?
- Do I think I will reach more people with a stall or with sponsorship?

Sponsoring can also often mean you don't need to go to the actual event you can just go for a short time to drop off brochures and banners. This way you can, by definition, be at several events on the same day because you're a sponsor not a stallholder.

If you have a stall and you get teachers or friends to 'man' it all day you may need to pay them, provide them with lunch and even travel money or t-shirts and these are additional costs you need to factor in when deciding whether to do the stall.

Have a good think, budget everything and then decide which option to go ahead with.

An Alternative To A Stall Or Sponsorship - Offer A Free Activity

Instead of a stall or sponsorship you could just use your time as your contribution and simply offer the organizers one of the following types of activities:

Free:
- Face painting
- Crèche/play area supervision (based on your credentials and working with children check and insurance)
- Craft demonstrations
- Dance Classes each hour on the hour for 20 minutes
- Magic show/entertainment

You can offer a service or activity for free and in return you can request that you have your pull up banners and flyers nearby to be able to advertise your business.

This is great for you because you don't have to pay the stall or sponsorship fee and the organizers love this because they get a useful value-adding activity or service, which enhances or helps the event and they haven't had to pay for it. It is a win-win arrangement that helps everyone: you, the organizers and the people coming to the event.

This particular type of option is very good specifically for charities where there is often pressure on the budget, plus you are being very generous and approachable as you've given your time and service free. This builds positive relationships and is good for your positive public relations.

Dance Shop Partnership

Your relationship with the local dance shop/s is really important. Not only do they help you, you help them. It is a win-win relationship. You can send all your new students and current students needing shoes and dancewear directly to these shops. You need to alert the dance shops to this by:

1. Asking your parents to mention your dance school's name when they go into the dance shop. This reinforces to the dance shop owner exactly where their customers are coming from. Also tell your parents that "Mrs Jones in the dance shop knows exactly what our students need for their classes."

2. You can email the dance shops personally at the beginning of each year and mid year basically checking in to see how they are going. You can send them your latest timetable showing what types of classes

you are offering. You can ask if they have any promotions/offers they are running that you could promote in your next dance school newsletter.

3. Drop into the dance shops once a term or so with some of your latest flyers, or an offer and pick up some of their business cards or flyers to display at your school.

4. All these things build positive working relationships with other businesses in the community and that is always good for everyone concerned. Positive relationships also lead to referrals.

Kids Online Directories (FREE)

The more you are visible on the internet promoting your brand, classes and offers the more you will increase your search engine rankings and increase the likelihood of showing on page one of Google or appearing in any search that someone does. List yourself on every free business listing you can find. Some of the directories (in Australia) you can start with are:

- Yalwa
- Hotfrog
- True Local
- Gumtree
- Activities 4 Kids
- Active Activities
- Bub Hub

There is a lot of debate around whether paid listings are effective. One way to find out is to go onto a paid site, find some businesses that are listed, ring them up and be very open and transparent and ask how effective their paid ads have been and how many customers they got from the ad.

I have done this and asked around a fair number of business owners and they have not seen a return on investment on paid directory advertising so I chose not to do it. It is up to you to do your own research and then you can decide if it could work for you in your area. See what your market research tells you.

Paying to be in someone else's newsletter

Directories and businesses that have a large list/database of people in the same target market as you may approach you to advertise in their newsletter for a fee. You may even do the same and approach other similar businesses with an offer for them to pay a fee to advertise in your newsletter.

Again you need to shop around to see if this is viable. Sign up to their newsletter and see what you think of it. Call up some of the current advertisers and ask them how it's working for them.

Key questions to ask the person offering you this option:

For communication effectiveness, ask questions in a friendly, open and inquiring way.

1. How many subscribers are on your list/database receiving the newsletter?

2. Where are these people located? (If they're not located near where your classes are based there's no point listing)
3. What's the 'open rate' of your newsletter (how many people open it)?
4. Do you know how other advertisers have gone in terms of responses from being in your newsletter?
5. Have you promoted a similar business to mine in the last 3 months?

If you do decide to give this a go make sure you include a compelling offer so that the subscribers are interested to learn more and take action.

Note: I tried this marketing strategy with a website focused on kids and Mums with a target group in the state I had dance classes running in. I did a free tutu offer if they enrolled via the newsletter advert. I got nothing, zilch, no response at all.

This is not to say they don't work, everything is worth a try. Who knows you might find one that is fabulous but do your research carefully, ask questions and keep the outlay costs low to minimize your risk initially.

Referrals

One of the best and most effective ways to encourage new parents to bring their children along to classes is if a mum mentions your classes to mums while waiting at the school gate, the mothers group or the Sunday BBQ. One way you can organize referrals is to have a 'bring a friend for free' system. If a current student brings their friend along the friend doesn't have to pay they can just try the class out.

Some teachers experiment with giving gifts or free classes to the mum/friend who referred the new friend but I have found this not to work as sometimes people feel insincere, feeling as if they're recommending something to someone and then getting a pay off to do it and it makes them feel uncomfortable. You may find small gifts work but it would need to be subtle and elegant in approach.

Another fabulous way to generate referrals is to open the invitation up when you have a showcase/demonstration or recital. Encourage current students to invite friends and family and neighbors to come along and see the performance, this generates a great feeling of community and other mums and young children see the classes and experience the studio and meet you.

PROMOTIONS

Most people have a rough idea of what a promotion is, as it was stated earlier, a promotion is a communication tool that gets your business message and offering out into the market place and more specifically hits your target market right between the eyes.

So when they think, "I want to send my child to dance classes" they think of you. It's normally a one-off type of activity; you may do it every year, every term etc but generally it lasts for a short space of time and then finishes. This is what makes it different to marketing. Marketing is consistent brand building, promotions are a spike in activity and then it dies down again and the marketing continues on.

What sorts of activities are really going to help get your business and your message out there? Below is a list of a few ways you could promote your business. Try some from the list below plus some of your own (be as creative as you can).

Promotional Activities:

- Launch – opening night, enrolment day
- Advertising in newspapers or magazines
- Merchandise
- Stand/stall at dance expo or fete
- Christmas events for charity
- Vehicle signage with offer
- TV opportunity
- Radio interview on community radio (most radio advertising is a high-cost, risky investment so I'd advise against that unless you had a fantastic deal or have a lot of cash to risk)
- Small touring show with your older/elite students
- Billboard signage
- Performance in schools/ pre-schools/ shopping centers/ fetes
- Direct Mail - brochure drop with offer
- Giveaways aligned with another business
- Website offers
- Networking at specific events

After the promotion, calculate the income you made from it in terms of direct enrolments and sales minus the outgoings and this will give you your return on investment (ROI), which is the actual amount you made from the promotion. Initially this could be quite low. Over time you will refine your promotional activities to be more lucrative.

Promotional activities generate both direct income e.g. selling goods on a stall but also generate increased enrolments, which lead to increased income for you.

Students who enroll in the period after a promotion should be asked where they heard about your school, and the enrolments which directly resulted from the promotional activity should be recorded as a good return on investment (ROI).

PARENT SURVEYS

Surveys are great for market research. I just conducted one for over 100 dance teachers and got some great responses that will really help me shape my mentoring programs. Surveys can return very insightful comments and great feedback for you!

- Run a free survey of 10 or less questions via Survey Monkey at the end of every year. Put the survey link in the newsletter, on the Facebook page and then send it out to individuals if you want to increase the number of respondents

- Only send to people who have completed either one or two full terms

- Ask questions that you need and want answers to. This can really shape the way to run classes. Everything from which days and times suit you best, to prices, holiday classes, other dance styles they'd be interested in and more.

- Make the questions specific – general questions give general answers whereas more specific questions give you answers that you can actually turn into action.

- Always make sure surveys are anonymous. You don't want respondents to "people please" and not be truthful because they know you know what they said.

RE-ENROLMENTS REMINDER MARKETING VIA EMAIL

On the Monday of week 9 send out 'Priority Re-Enrolment' emails to all parents of currently enrolled students explaining that in 14 days (give the exact date) places will be opened up to the waiting lists and the general public. This gives you ALL of week 9 and week 10 to enroll as many existing students as possible.

This method acknowledges and respects the loyalty of your existing customers by making them a priority over new people. It also stops new students taking the place of existing students and possibly creating conflicts when classes get full.

Monday of week 1 of the school holidays (14 days after the "Priority Re-Enrolment" email) open up enrolments to the waiting lists and the public. This then gives you two full weeks of the holidays to fill all unfilled places with new people.

This means the re-enrolment plus new enrolment period covers a 4-week time period. This is a great way to gauge your numbers but also creates this "trickle" effect so you're not bombarded with enrolments all in a couple of days at the beginning of term.

Inform all customers of re-enrolment or enrolment information via email first. It's free and easy to get quick responses. If people don't respond to the initial email send a "48 hours to close of priority enrolment" email to people who haven't responded.

Then as the term starts to edge towards starting date give non-responding people a phone call directly. Often they have been away or just too busy and have not got around to enrolling.

WORD OF MOUTH MARKETING – STILL THE MOST POPULAR!

I recently conducted a survey of 100 dance teachers currently operating dance studios. This survey was national and pulled research from small and large dance schools right across Australia. The results regarding marketing were astounding.

Way, way out in front was WOM – word of mouth marketing followed by parent referrals which are also based on word of mouth methods. What astounded me was in this day and age where everyone is talking about social media and new technology to build brands, the most old fashioned of them all was the most popular.

So here are 3 tips to keep up the Word of Mouth Marketing

- **Keep in touch with your parents over the summer break** - don't end up wondering if people will enrol on time when they haven't heard from you over the break. You need to be 'Top of Mind' in their mind when it comes to re-enrolling, telling their friends about new classes in the New Year and any additional styles you have starting. Your Mailchimp newsletter is a great way of doing this.

- **Be unique** – People remark on things that are remarkable! It's so important that certain classes/comps/additional activities you have starting or happening are amplified and well branded!

- **Get people talking** – online or via your newsletter or website/social media try running a competition, cook off, photo competition or anything where people get involved and get talking!

The key to marketing mastery is to never stop! Keep doing it and doing it and doing it! The more you're reminding people of you and your school the better!

In Summary...

- Marketing is not promotions
- Marketing is about consistency, consistency, consistency
- Marketing effectiveness comes from a multi-pronged marketing approach
- The marketing mix is both online and offline
- Marketing is what drives sales

CHAPTER 3

THE DANCE PROGRAM

AN EXCELLENT AND EFFECTIVE DANCE PROGRAM IS REALLY CRIT-
ical for you in your dance studio. If you think about the many
dance industry bodies for example RAD, ISTD, Cecchetti and
more - they all have their own original dance programs. A
program is professional, structured and has outcomes and
rewards for the children. If we want to take our schools up
a notch we really need to be incorporating programs.

Parents see the value in programs, the gradation of classes
and outcome based activities. Whether they are consciously
aware of it or not, the pure fact that there is a program with
a process means they will take your school more seriously
because they perceive you and your studio to be more valuable in its offering compared to other studios.

This will also lead to customers being much more likely to pay you higher fees because of the 'value-perception' being created as a result of developing and implementing programs in your studio.

In the branding module you would've created and come up with some names and logos for your classes. Have the name, the brand, the feel and the culture in mind when you are creating your dance program. To create an excellent dance program we need to be incorporating 4 Key Elements.

1. Fun & joyful
2. Structured
3. Engaging
4. Outcomes based

Fun & Joyful

The dance program you create needs to be fun, joyful and creative. If the children absolutely love the program, exercises and dances they will want to come back and this is great news for you! It also makes the program wonderful for you to teach which means you will show up with more energy and enthusiasm plus when you have other teachers teaching the program they will love it too and will also be enthusiastic to teach the children your program.

Structured

No programs work effectively unless they are structured. There really has to be a fantastic, tight structure so that what sits within the program works and produces results for you and the children. Children also need a lot of structure to feel in control and this is also a great way to incorporate early philosophies of self-discipline, working towards end goals and the early understanding and introduction of delayed gratification.

Engaging

The program you create needs to be very engaging, meaning that it is designed and developed with the children in mind. Their age, stage, level of understanding and abilities need to be well thought out. There needs to also be a good amount of change, style and scene setting so the children stay focused and engaged on you.

Outcomes Based

I believe that all people, starting from a young age should be acknowledged for the hard work they put into any activity. The incorporation of outcomes and then a reward is really useful. The written outcomes are also for the parents to see what their child is learning, developing in and achieving and the reward at the end of the term or semester is to acknowledge them for their hard work and commitment.

Certificates

To tie in directly with outcomes based work, I created the Demonstration Day Certificate, which meant that at the end of every term, in week 10, the children would present their learned work for that term to family and friends.

Certificates were presented individually to each child on the day. The learning outcomes for that term were written on the back of the certificate so parents could see what the students had learnt.

If you go to the Fairy Footsteps Facebook page and scroll through the photos you will see many images of the little ballerinas holding their certificates.

Developing the Program

STAGE 1

Paper/Whiteboard - Get out a big piece of butchers paper or use a whiteboard

Age Group - Think about the age of the group you are developing your program for. Write their age at the top of the page.

Dance Style – Write the dance style next to the age.

Brainstorm – In a long list think of ALL the dance movements, steps or techniques that you think this age can do based on your previous teaching experience.

Top 40 – Develop a list of the top 40 movements or skills you believe are age appropriate.

Note – Next to each movement or step write what you believe is the easiest and hardest. You may decide to write an 'e' next to things that are fairly easy, an 'm' for things that are medium and an 'h' for things you think are harder but within the year of the program the children should be able to master.

Here's an example with the e, m and h listed next to the exercise:

- Skips | M
- Gallops | H
- Kicks | E
- Sways | E
- Tendus | M
- Sautés | E
- Walks | E
- Pony Gallops | H
- Walks on demi point | M

Note – children of a young age are attempting these new exercises and techniques so they will by no means be competent, we are allowing them to experience and demonstrate to us that they are 'having a go' and 'feeling it out'.

Children learn from observing and then attempting the step themselves, that is, seeing someone demonstrate the steps correctly and then having a go themselves even if they can't do the steps. The observing and the repetition is what count.

STAGE 2

Divide - Divide the list of 40 up into groups of 10, containing some easy, some medium and some hard from your list. We are going by Australian yearly terms of which there are 4. This structure can work for semesters or other study periods as well.

You should now have 4 lists with 10 steps on each list.

Ballet Class Structure - We are now going to categorize your first list of 10 steps into the traditional classical ballet class structure. I am Royal Academy of Dance trained so I will be referring to that model. You may have another method as a reference guide and that's fine as well.

1. Centre work - eg pliés, tendus, sautés, clapping exercises
2. Corner/diagonal work - eg skips, gallops, walks, kicks
3. Circle work - eg tucked runs, runs on demi point,
4. Dances - eg combinations, drama incorporated, improvisation
5. Curtsey

Note: for the preschool age I don't do any barre work. You may choose to incorporate some basics or some stretches at the barre with your young ones. If you are operating out of a school hall or community hall you may not have access to a ballet barre and that's fine.

Looking at my ballet class structure list and the examples, place your chosen steps in the sections of the ballet class structure where you believe they would fit.

Music – I advise people to find the music first and then choreograph the exercise, otherwise, you think up this fabulous exercise only to discover there's no music to match. You may buy and find music from iTunes, on CD or any other music provider. Listen to lots of tracks suitable for this age group and start to decide which tracks would work for certain types of steps, eg skips would be upbeat and fairly fast timing, whereas a piece for plies needs to be slow and measured.

I encourage teachers to use a range of music from classical, musical theatre, instrumental – depending on what dance style you're focusing on, make sure you really mix up the music choices to keep it fascinating and interesting for the children.

STAGE 3

Props - Children absolutely *love* props. Props really anchor the exercises into the child's mind, they enhance the exercise and they generate an element of story and drama into exercises, which is essential for this age group. Props also really help children to remember the exercise as they associate a certain prop with a certain exercise.

I found when I was developing my program I couldn't be too picky and choosy on what props to use, because you may come up with a fabulous idea for a prop to match a certain step only to find out after searching high and low and online you simply can't find the prop! This becomes very frustrating.

My advice would be – either (1) go to the store or online and have a look at types of props you could use and then develop the drama and the choreography around the prop or (2) Incorporate really standard props like scarves, bags, wands and teddy bears – the kinds of things that are always available.

*Important - make sure props are child-safe. Most toys/props from toy stores will be ok and most of the time they say 'For children 3 and up' which is good. Make sure you find the label that says that. For children under 3 I would advise only using props like scarves, streamers, soft cushions, round bouncy balls. Avoid using any props with little bits and pieces that can flick off, have pointy or jagged ends or even toys with eyes can be a problem as they can pop out or flick off and a child could pop that in their mouth in class without you noticing and this could be very dangerous.

Choreography – to choreograph the exercises I advise people to hire out a school hall or somewhere similar if you don't have a big room at home. You really need a good amount of space with no distractions so you can completely lose yourself in the creativity and flow of your choreography.

Each creation of an exercise should take about 15 minutes because you already have the step, the prop and the music ready. The actual choreography of the step being turned into an exercise can become very quick, sometimes within a couple of minutes you will come up with something good.

I created my year-long program over about 3 days. I had already chosen the props and the music so when I came to devise the choreography it really wasn't too time consuming.

Turning a Step Into An Exercise
1. Take your first list of 10 steps written down
2. Choose one type of step eg. skips
3. Look at the choices of music you have for this step
4. Look at the props you have that can work with this step

5. Choose your track, the step and the structure of where it is going to be (center, corner, circle or a dance etc) then just go! Just start seeing what starts to flow with the music and the prop you've chosen.

6. Do this for all the remaining 9 steps on your list and then you have created 10 exercises! Video all the exercises when you have choreographed them (see the videoing notes at end of this module).

STAGE 4

The Program Structure – Once all 40 exercises have been created into 4 batches of 10 with a nice variety of steps, music, props and center, corner, circle and dance work you should now have in front of you these 4 lists that are named and have corresponding music.

Each list becomes 1 week of work for the children. Eg List 1 is Week 1, List 2 is Week 2 and so on.

1. Class Structure

This is an example of the class structure for week 1. As you can see the 10 exercises cover center, corner and dances work.

1. Introduction
- Welcome Circle
- Stretches

2. Centre
- Plies
- Spring points
- Kneeling Port de Bras
- It's Time to Clean Up (Feather Duster Prop)

- Whistle While you Work
- Flying Dance

3. Corner

- Walk & Point through the Flowers
- Step and Kick from the Corner
- Sparkle Skips around Sparkle (Pom Pom)

4. Dances

Demi Character - Drama themed exercises

- It's Your Special Day Parade

Dance Improvisation

- Free Dance

5. Finish

- Curtsey/Bow & Sticker

2. Introduction - As you can see I have a welcome circle at the beginning. This is where at the beginning of every class, as the children file in, we sit down in a circle together (teacher too) and we build rapport, collect ourselves and make the children feel comfortable.

We ask them how their day is and we can also encourage them to introduce themselves to the group. Go around each child and ask them to say their name in a loud voice "Hi everyone, I'm Monica!"

At the end, you can get the children to clap as everyone has been confident and brave.

3. Finish – I encourage all children to learn how to execute a proper curtsey or bow. This introduces them to the fact that this is how dance classes end. We do this at the end of every class.

I then get the children to line up in a straight, calm line and then they receive a sticker on their hand for doing a good job in class. (only for 3year old and up) If you think the children have not behaved today, you may choose not to give them a sticker. This is up to you.

The Dance Manual

Producing a dance manual of the exercises you have created is really useful; not only for you to continue to make improvements, but also if you want to employ other teachers either straight away or later down the track it is so easy. You can simply give them the manual to read through. When you have teacher meetings and modify or discuss the program you can all refer to the manual.

Manuals do make for a professionally run show! You can also show new parents the manual, which outlines what the children will learn and the outcomes they will receive from doing your program.

1. I had 4 manuals (Week 1, Week 2, Week 3 and Week 4), printed and bound –1 manual for each week of 10 exercises. I used my local Officeworks store for very inexpensive printing.

2. The example below shows how 2 exercises have been written out in the manual.

Example of two exercises from manual:

Spring Points

1. Starting in first position
2. Spring points x 16
3. Clap x 8
4. Repeat all

Kneeling Port de Bras

Kneeling either on the mat or anywhere in the room, even in a circle

- Lift arms over head and cross at wrists with body bent right over knees
- Come up and open arms out to sides and down
- Repeat, lifting arms up over head and bending over knees and crossing wrists
- Lift up and sway side to side with arms over head and wilting over and bending each side x 4
- Sit on left buttock and external right leg and do swan arms x 2 – undulate, undulate
- Come back to the center and repeat on right hand side with left leg extended
- Finish either with the extended leg or back to the center lifting up and finishing bent over knees with wrists crossed

How to use the program in the term

The way I developed the program meant that for each week we would work from the manual that corresponds to that week. We would then repeat 2 weeks and then focus on one weeks work for that term. I know it sounds a bit confusing and you may work out a better system that works for you and your team of teachers. This worked well for us and this is how it looked:

TERM 1

PROGRAM FOR TERM 1 (Week 1 Focus)	SCHOOL TERM WEEKS
Week 1 Program Manual	1
Week 2 Program Manual	2
Week 3 Program Manual	3
Week 4 Program Manual	4
Week 1 Program Manual	5
Week 2 Program Manual	6
Week 1 Program Manual	7
(focus week Term 1) **Week 1 Program Manual**	8
(focus week Term 1) **Week 1 Program Manual**	9
(focus week Term 1) **Week 1 Program Manual**	10
DEMONSTRATION DAY	

TERM 2

PROGRAM FOR TERM 2	SCHOOL
(Week 2 Focus)	TERM WEEKS
Week 1 Program Manual	1
Week 2 Program Manual	2
Week 3 Program Manual	3
Week 4 Program Manual	4
Week 2 Program Manual	5
Week 3 Program Manual	6
Week 2 Program Manual	**7**
(focus week Term 2)	
Week 2 Program Manual	**8**
(focus week Term 2)	
Week 2 Program Manual	**9**
(focus week Term 2)	
Week 2 Program Manual	**10**
DEMONSTRATION DAY	

TERM 3

PROGRAM FOR TERM 3	SCHOOL
(Week 3 Focus)	TERM WEEKS
Week 1 Program Manual	1
Week 2 Program Manual	2
Week 3 Program Manual	3
Week 4 Program Manual	4
Week 3 Program Manual	5
Week 4 Program Manual	6
Week 3 Program Manual	7
(focus week Term 3)	
Week 3 Program Manual	8
(focus week Term 3)	
Week 3 Program Manual	9
(focus week Term 3)	
Week 3 Program Manual	10
DEMONSTRATION DAY	

TERM 4

PROGRAM FOR TERM 4	SCHOOL
(Week 4 Focus)	TERM WEEKS
Week 1 Program Manual	1
Week 2 Program Manual	2
Week 3 Program Manual	3
Week 4 Program Manual	4
Week 1 Program Manual	5
Week 2 Program Manual	6
Week 4 Program Manual	**7**
(focus week Term 4)	
Week 4 Program Manual	**8**
(focus week Term 4)	
Week 4 Program Manual	**9**
(focus week Term 4)	
Week 4 Program Manual	**10**
DEMONSTRATION DAY	

This adds variety for the children by incorporating a range of work but it also means that in the term they are demonstrating the work that corresponds to the term they are in and they get 5-6 opportunities during the term to practice it! Children do love to repeat work so they can master it, don't get concerned that they need to be doing or learning new material all the time. This is how they learn – by repetition.

VIDEO YOUR CHOREOGRAPHY

I also decided to video myself during the time I was choreographing to demonstrate the exercises with the props and to the music. This was so useful for when I needed to remember what I'd created and then when I went on and taught my teachers the program they all had the video available on a private YouTube channel to remind themselves.

Also, when I sold the business I was able to give the new owner all the videos and she has been able to use them to further recruit teachers and be reminded of exercises. Videoing has been very useful and helpful for retaining the integrity of the original program.

I simply used my iPad on some piled up chairs and then easily uploaded the exercises straight to YouTube. I'm not 'techy' and I didn't have a professional camera and it still worked really well, so don't be discouraged if you don't have the right equipment, just do your best and it's usually fine with the technology we have available these days.

In Summary...

- **Make your program structured, fun, joyful, engaging and outcomes based**
- **Music first, steps and props second**
- **Props and themes anchor children**
- **Repetition is good and helpful for their learning**
- **Certificates or ribbons for acknowledgement**
- **Dance manuals and videos for teachers**

CHAPTER 4

TEACHERS AND TRAINING

THE PEOPLE IN YOUR BUSINESS WHETHER IT'S DANCE OR ANY-
thing else can really make or break your business. Whether
you're running your school as a single operator and you do
everything from teaching to tax or whether you employ
people – it's the people (that includes you) that make all the
difference.

Dance is a skill and the type of business we're in to deliver
that skill is class based with ourselves teaching or teachers
under our employ. Essentially this is a 'people based business.' It's so important for us to be discerning about our own
best practice, our own presentation, delivery and teaching
style.

We also need to be most discerning regarding the people
we employ. Your people are your ambassadors; they represent your brand, your school and you.

From my years of work in this industry I have discovered there are usually two levels of teachers:

1. Competent
2. Excellent

Anyone who is less than competent shouldn't be under your employ. What we are aiming to do is shift people who work for us from being competent to being excellent. Once this happens certain things begin to change in your studio including:

- Students stay and re-enroll
- Parents are impressed by your teachers
- Your school and classes gain a strong reputation
- Other teachers approach you and want to work for you
- The teacher's commitment and professionalism is second to none
- You don't have to worry about how your teachers will relate to parents or students

Having excellent teaches will turn your business around. Your staff will become an asset to your business and there is incredible value in that, especially if you have a vision to grow your studio.

If you want to grow your studio you can only be in one place at one time therefore you need to be able to rely on your teachers who are representing you. Does this mean they need to be at an elite professional level? Does this mean they need to be a prima ballerina or have been a back-up dancer for Beyoncé? The answer is: No Way! What they do need however is a pure love of children and dance.

Teacher Capability Example

COMPETENT TEACHER	EXCELLENT TEACHER
Skilled at dance	Skilled at dance
Interested in teaching	Enthusiastic about teaching
Likes children	Loves children
Waits for you to organize everything	Takes charge and takes control of their classes
Nice to parents	Friendly, warm and welcoming to parents
Turns up and does the job	Loves the job and "goes the extra mile"
Teaches students well	Nurtures, listens and tends to individuals
Represents studio professionally	Is an "ambassador" for your studio

The competent teacher is nice, reliable and does an OK job. The excellent teacher loves the job; they love their role as a dance teacher and see it as something to be proud of.

So you ask - Won't this teacher leave me and set up their own school if they're that fabulous?

The answer to this is yes and no. The yes answer means that when you interview them, try to get to know them as a person and not just whether they can do the job. If you have taught them yourself you have sussed them out from what they've said and implied whether running their own school is something they would like to do. If this seems to be something they're really keen on you really have to consider whether you will take them on.

However, there are many ways to have teachers work for you who see you operate your business so seamlessly that even if they wanted to run their own school they wouldn't know how. People will often hold back and not pursue things when it comes to the "how". They know they should, they know they could but they just don't know "how" or they don't want to.

If teachers who work for you have so much trust, faith and confidence in you they will perceive you as an expert at running a school and believe me, it will take a lot for them to go out on their own and start up as the competition and risk everything.

What makes a teacher leave you and operate under his or her own name and brand?

Let's face it some teachers are ambitious and they want to set up their own school. This is a fact of life. However, some teachers can feel they want to set up their own school because they are not satisfied with their position as a teacher and feel they would like to run their own show. To reduce the chance of this dissatisfaction starting and building up try to avoid the following.

Dissatisfaction can happen when teachers:
1. Are disappointed with how things are run at your school
2. Feel the classes they've been given are too demanding and challenging

3. Don't feel listened to or understood by you
4. Don't believe they are paid well enough for what they do
5. Feel they have to do things outside their job description
6. Lack faith in your leadership capacity
7. Are sick of "parents and politics"
8. Feel ill informed and out-of-the-loop

If you sense that some of these points ring true for you and how some of your past or present teachers feel you need to take the time to really reassess the way you operate with teachers.

What makes excellent teachers stay with you:

1. They are carefully chosen based on their enthusiasm and love of children and not just dance skills and CV.
2. You run such a tight ship that they feel solid and secure working for you.
3. You inspire confidence in them.
4. Your business is so well run they don't know how you do it so well and think they couldn't possibly do it like you do.
5. They are paid on time, every time.
6. They love your faith in them to deliver and you don't micro-manage them.
7. They don't feel out of their depth. They know exactly what's expected of them and what they're meant to teach.
8. There is a teacher's handbook/manual that outlines the whole way you run your studio.
9. You keep up weekly communication/check-ins and face-to-face meetings with them.

10. You have training each year and face-to-face meetings at the beginning of every term so everyone feels in the loop.

I have worked across dance, performing arts and children's entertainment and I have employed a variety of people. Most recently I had two teachers working for me on the other side of the country and I found them to be excellent with rave reviews from parents.

The reason I got these results was because I focused on drawing out their excellence and by training them, providing them with the environment that made them feel respected, professional, looked after and a vital part of the dance school.

Loyalty

These days a lot of people say that employees are not loyal. But if you look at a lot of workplaces, would you be loyal? Loyalty is created and earned by the people running the business and if it's really good then people won't leave because they know that somewhere else won't be as good. When I was running Fairy Footsteps I even had teachers from other preschool ballet studios ring me and submit CVs and want to come and work for me because they were so impressed with the way I operated.

Key factors that build loyal employees:

- Respect for them

- Acknowledgement of their work and contribution

- Listened to by you and their thoughts taken into account

1. Respect

Respect is something that every single person on the planet wants. Wars, gangs, divorces and self-destruction often spring from a feeling of lack of respect for self and/or others. If you demonstrate to your teachers that you respect them, you will keep them.

How:

- Pay them for training
- Pay them for any admin/phone calls
- Ask them what their thoughts are about classes and students
- Take their views of parent dynamics seriously
- Ask them when they would like you to intervene with a situation - don't just assume you should or you shouldn't
- Let them know of any changes as early as possible
- Don't hide the truth from them
- Be transparent about their performance in a non-personal objective way

2. Acknowledgement

Acknowledgement is another word for "thank you". It really is about showing your manners and being prepared to thank people for the work they do. When people feel acknowledged they actually work harder and they want to impress you because, like any psychological trigger, when they do a good job you acknowledge them. This makes them feel good so they want to do a good job again.

How:

- Say "thank you" in person

- Include thanks in emails/texts/phone calls

- Give a little gift at the end of term/birthday/Christmas

- Send kind words/testimonials from parents through to teachers

- Talk about and thank teachers on social media

- Thank them at Demonstration Days and concerts

- Talk to the parents about how fabulous your teachers are

- Sign off newsletters from you and your teachers

- Don't make any teacher feel any less important or more important than others - in other words - Don't have favorites

3. Listened to

Dance teachers are creative and they may have ideas for things within classes and choreographically and that's fantastic. They are also on the frontline. They are at the "coal face" which means they see everything that's happening. What's happening at the venue, timeslots, parents interactions, student interest etc so It's crucial to take their ideas and observations on board.

How:

1. Have a monthly face to face meeting with each teacher individually and ask them what they're noticing

2. Make them feel really comfortable. Say you won't be offended by anything they say, you'd just rather know

3. Ask them to be honest about different parents, children, class sizes, class times, noise, the studio and so on

Your teachers are your primary way of getting "in" on what's really going on in classes that you're not attending or teaching yourself

4. Thoughts & Ideas

Once you gain feedback from teachers and you know what's going on make sure you follow through because one of the most frustrating things for employees is when the "boss" (you) says they're interested in the employees' ideas and input and is ready to listen only to smile, nod and do nothing. It's crucial that if you gain insights and it's at all possible to implement changes based on these insights that you actually do something! Become someone who follows through! If you can't, then tell the teacher why. This builds trust and respect - the backbone of successful relationships.

Teachers or employees who take advantage of you

Sometimes we think someone is perfect and they really match our criteria with a CV to boot. Later we find out that they are actually taking advantage of us. They are using their position to manipulate or disrespect in perhaps a passive aggressive way or another way. I advise having all teachers on an initial 3-month probation. I say this is a two-way probation where they have as much right as me to decide if they want to continue or not. This way, after 3 months you can sit them down and objectively express why they wont be continuing at your studio.

Code of Conduct

Create your own Code of Conduct for the people who work with you. Your code is based on your philosophy and values so they shouldn't change. Aim for no more than ten. You need to include the Code of Conduct in your Teachers Manual and in your Student/Parent handbook if you decide to create one.

Recruitment

Often as dance teachers we have our senior students help us as assistants, they can then go on to teach for us for many years to come or we hear on the 'grapevine' that a local dancer is available to teach classes. But what if this doesn't happen? What if you are expanding and you need to recruit more teachers the more traditional way. There are certain key characteristics you need to keep in mind when you're making a new hire.

Teacher Profile

Outline the type of teacher you need by answering these questions:

- What age group will this teacher be teaching?
- How much technical skill do they need?

- What type of personality/animation and engagement level do they need to possess to teach this age group?
- How many years teaching experience do they need to have?
- What qualifications do they need?

Once you've identified in your mind the type of teacher you need you can then create the job advert based on the answers to those questions. Below is an exact job advert I used to recruit teachers.

Remember - Happy teachers are your best ambassadors. Ambassadors wave the flag for your school. They respect you and your school and they love working for you. The way to create enthusiastic ambassadors is through the communication you have with them, the respect you have for them and the belief you have in their work.

JOB ADVERT EXAMPLE

Preschool Ballet/Dance Teacher

- Do you have dance/movement skills?
- Experience working in a child related industry or experience dance teaching?

We are looking for people who have dance/movement skills. Previous dance teaching experience and experience in a child-related industry is highly regarded. We offer full training and provide all materials and mentoring.

Essential Requirements:

- Current drivers license and your own car

- Current Australian Business Number (ABN) or willing to get one
- Current Working with Children Check certificate or be willing to get one
- 3-5 years dance/movement experience
- Previous work in a child related industry

Hours of Work

- 9AM – 11AM (2hrs) Tuesday
- 3.30PM – 5.30PM (2hrs) Tuesday

Initial Weekly Total:

Hours: 4 hours work (minimum)

Payment: $40 per hour. $160 per week (minimum)

JOB COMMENCEMENT: Term 1 February 2014

POSITION DESCRIPTION

Working with Us

- We provide full training
- We provide props, music, dance manual & training
- You don't buy anything from us or pay for training with us
- We aim to work with you in and around the times that work for you
- Head office manages all enrollments/accounts and mass marketing
- We remunerate you every fortnight

What's Expected of You:

- A genuine interest and love of children and teaching

- Follow all guidelines of employment as per Fairy Footsteps agreement and associated documents

- Possess a responsible, punctual and ethical way of working

- Attend regular teacher meetings

- Perform as a committed teacher of preschool ballet classes

TEACHING DANCE

A Fairy Footsteps teacher is fun, friendly and energetic. Our teachers have a love of dance and of preschool children. Seeing children develop, challenge themselves and learn is what excites our teachers.

What we're looking for in dance teachers:

- **Vibrant Personality** - An animated personality/teaching style

- **Teaching Experience or Qualifications** - Ballet/dance teaching experience or ballet teaching qualifications OR someone who's worked in early childhood education, fitness or preschool teaching and has some background in dance

- **Love of Children** - A love for and experience working with children aged 2 – 5 years

- **Communication Skills** - Good communication skills

RATE OF PAY FOR DANCE TEACHING

Initially $160 per week for 4hrs dance teaching.

Finding Teachers

If you're looking for teachers and you know people who would work well within the culture of your studio, that's excellent, but if you don't I would consider casting your net wide to see what other talent is out there. Free job listing sites are easy to use and you can target them by area too. Below are some Australian sites I have used to find dance teachers and entertainers.

Dance Informa

http://danceinforma.com.au/directories/dance-jobs/

Star Now

http://www.starnow.com.au/Casting-Calls/Dancers-wanted/Teachers/

Gumtree

http://www.gumtree.com.au/p-post-ad2.html

Pedestrian

https://www.pedestrian.tv/login/index.htm

I also had some quite good results when I listed on SEEK (Australia) but it is about $250 to list.

Collecting CVs

I have run adverts time and time again for teachers, assistants, entertainers and administrative people and you find you end up with a pile of CVs and you have to sift through them quickly to find the gems.

Quickly skim each CV and assess on the first look and gut instinct as to whether you like what you see/read. Trusting your gut instinct or intuition is an important part of this. If you just sense that a person could be right or not then take this into account as well as what is written.

Save the pile of CVs you like and go through each one and look the person up on Google, their website and Facebook etc. You can also look on YouTube and see if they have any videos of their work. Get a further feel for whether you think they would be a good match for your school's culture.

You should now have a 'shortlist' of between 5 and 10 CVs. Get in touch with these people and line up face-to-face interviews.

Key Tips for Interviewing

Interviewing is quite exhausting. People tend to underestimate how much energy and preparation it takes to interview, engage and assess the person sitting in front of them.

Allow 1 hour per interview - it really takes time to get comfortable, to ask questions carefully and to gauge how you think and feel about how a person will go. The more time you spend with the person the better you can assess them. For example some people are nervous at the beginning so if the interview is short they may not have time to relax and show you what they're really like.

Allow 30 mins between interviews - you really need time to gather yourself, freshen up and relax between each person and take notes on the interview you have just conducted. Sufficient breaks between interviews means each interview is of a better quality and you are more likely to make a better decision because you are not rushed and tired.

Make sure you've read the person's CV carefully. The 30 mins break gives you time to read the next person's CV through. It's important you're across what they've done and you can draw out questions based on their CV. Nothing is more annoying to an interviewee than being asked questions that make it obvious that the CV hasn't been read. For example 'How long did you teach at school A?' when the CV states clearly that they worked at school A for two years. When you've read the CV you would say 'I notice you've worked at school A for two years, can you tell me in detail what classes you were teaching there and how this developed your teaching skills.' Have a printed copy of their CV in front of you. This makes you look focused and engaged on their experience and background and makes it easy for you to refer to.

Only interview 4-6 people in a day. This is the maximum that I found I could interview and still be alert and engaged with. Spending an hour with people and asking similar questions and staying alert and on your game is tiring. You might get through more but I found 4-6 people were my ideal. Time wise if you spend 1 hour per interview with 30mins in between and preparation and tidy up - that will take most of a working day.

Interview in a relaxed environment - I would recommend a large, spacious cafe with some privacy e.g. booths (you want to minimize people overhearing) or in the studio. If you use your studio you can show them around too which is good and see how they respond to what they see and note what questions they ask. Some large hotels have foyers with lounges where people meet for business lunches, which can be both relaxed and business like.

If you use a cafe or hotel make sure it matches your brand values. An upmarket hotel foyer/lobby gives the impression you are sophisticated and upmarket so your studio should match those values. Wherever you choose to hold interviews is making an impression so just make sure that impression matches your studio's culture.

Make sure that the interviewee comes to you - In communication terms this indicates who has the power in the situation and that should be you as the employer. Whenever someone comes to you, you are in the power position, which is where you need to be when hiring.

If you are meeting outside the studio and you both have coffee/tea - you pay. Similarly with the location of the interview, the person who pays for the coffee holds the power. This is part of impression management. You need to offer a drink, order it and then pay or provide a drink if the interview is at your studio.

Refresh - this one's just thrown in for good measure. Between each interview be sure to check your teeth, hair, make-up and clothes. Update your lippy; pop a mint and a spritz of perfume. Also have a drink of water to stay hydrated. This will ensure you look and feel refreshed and revitalized.

Choosing attitude and Character over Skills - There have been many articles written about the value of hiring based on a person's attitude, values, good character and great personality over skills, qualifications and credentials. The last 3 aspects are important and need to be taken note of but the first 4 are what will make for an excellent teacher.

You want to employ people who are nice, good people, who are positive and enthusiastic with students and who are committed and hardworking. It goes without saying that there will be a level of professional criteria that is needed but once those essentials are ticked it's most important to be assessing the person on a 'personal fit' with your studio culture, your students, your teachers and you.

Personality Plus!!

From my experience hiring people in the performing arts industry you really want people with great personalities! You want upbeat, smiling, happy people who really love children, dance and teaching.

If you then want to add children's parties, drama, entertainment or events onto your dance school offerings these people can dovetail easily into these and help to expand your business into other areas that complement dance.

Probation Period

In my experience it's a good idea to have all new teachers on a 3-month probation period for you to assess them and them to assess you and your school. At the end of the 3 months, you both have the option to not continue and you both know this at the outset of hiring.

Contracts

Teachers can be hired as employees or on contract. If they are taken on as contractors they need a formal contract regardless of the number of hours they work. The contract needs to be drawn up by a solicitor or lawyer and outline everything about their employment, hours, conditions and pay etc. In the contract have a section about the probation period, what happens at the end of that and also about continuing employment after this period.

Give the contract to the teacher at the beginning when you hire them, before they start on the probation period so that they can have time to read it through and get their solicitor or lawyer to read it too before it is signed and before they start working for you. If teachers are not taken on as employees then make sure they have a contract at all times to protect both them and you and reduce the risk of problems and disputes.

Note: There are legal obligations around different contracts, employers, workers compensation, superannuation and more. Be sure to discuss all these rules and regulations with your solicitor and accountant so you are legally covered.

Pay Scale

If you want great teachers they will come at a price, however you can also have a sliding scale, which is graded on experience and length of service. You may choose to have all teachers with professional teaching certification from a dance institution paid at X amount and other teachers without this certification at a lesser amount.

Some people might grade payment on years of teaching experience e.g. up to 5 years teaching experience gets X amount, 5-10 years get another amount and 10 years plus gets the highest. Some people have all teachers on the same pay scale. It all depends on your teachers, your views about pay scales, your cash flow, the size of your school and any industry pay awards that might stipulate payment at a certain minimum for certain training and experience.

Keep in mind that people feel valued by the way they are treated and the rate they are paid. You can't expect to get loyal, highly skilled teachers if you pay them the minimum rate.

Sample Questions I Ask in Interviews:
1. What attracted you to this particular job?
2. What style and type of teacher are you? Describe your teaching style for me.
3. Which age group/s do you love to teach and why?
4. What in your life do you consider you have a long-term commitment to?
5. What do you love about dance?
6. What do you love about children?
7. What do you love about teaching?
8. What's the focus in your life right now?

9. Do you see yourself some day running your own school?
10. How do you deal with challenging students? Give me examples
11. Describe the relationship you have with parents
12. How do you deal with challenging parents? Give me examples
13. What are your three favorite books and why are they your favorites?
14. Describe for me a challenging teaching experience you have had and how you dealt with it
15. Describe for me a fantastic teaching experience or achievement you have had
16. What are the three most important qualities that make an outstanding dance teacher and why those three?
17. How do you intend to develop yourself further as a dance teacher?
18. What will your life look like three years from now?

How to decide on interviewees based on attitude and character

Key questions to ask yourself post interview:

- What's your first feeling about the person after reading their CV and then meeting them in person?

- Did they seem false and superficial in the interview? Do you think they said what they thought you'd want to hear? Did they seem rehearsed? Or did they seem genuine and open in their answers to your questions?

- Were they gracious, warm, well mannered and respectful or did they seem egotistical, pushy or demanding? If they were, this is disrespectful to you and your position as the Studio Director so how do you think they would be as a staff member?

- Were they relaxed after they got over any initial nervousness? Or were they fidgety or anxious? This can mean they are unsure or maybe unfocused.

- What is their main focus in life at the moment? Family? Study? Another job? Auditions? Their answers will help you to assess their potential commitment or loyalty.

- Did they present well overall? Notice the small details e.g. chipped nail polish, sloppy dress or clean nails and tidy hair. These details give you an idea of their professionalism and personal standards. These standards will be brought to their work.

- Did they arrive late? This one is very important especially in the line of work you want them to do. Their punctuality will demonstrate to you how organized they are in their professional life.

- Their carriage? What's their level of poise and posture? Do they walk with good posture? Did they sit appropriately? This can indicate their level of confidence and how they will come across to parents, students and other teachers.

- Their responses. Did they answer in an articulate way? Were their answers thoughtful and responsible or short and unsure or confused?

- Their sense of humor and manner. Did they have a pleasant 'up' energy with a dash of humor? Or did they seem very serious with a 'down' energy? Working in dance with children it's important to have an energy and manner that keeps the children engaged and interested. A sense of humor is important.

Use the above as a checklist after each interview. Quickly jot down your responses so that you record them as soon as possible after meeting the person. With too much time between interviews these things can be forgotten.

Ultimate Organization

The most efficient and effective way to run your studio and to ensure teachers are on the 'same page' as you and each other is to have certain manuals and information. Firstly, I'm going to talk about the Preschool Ballet Program Teacher Training Information Manual. This Manual ensures that all teachers are aware of how to set up their room for classes, checklists for opening and pack up and a reminder of balletic technique and glossary so everyone is using the correct terminology. Please use this example as a guideline for your own studio and start handing them out to teachers as soon as possible.

EXAMPLE

Preschool Ballet Program Teacher Training Information Manual

Insert your Copyright Statement and Disclaimer here

It is best to seek legal advice on the wording of these.

ABC DANCE SCHOOL

'Nurturing your child's imagination & creativity through ballet & drama'

MISSION

Write your Mission Statement here

VISION

Write your Vision Statement here

AIM

Write the Aim of your dance studio here

INTRODUCTION

The XXX program is designed to inspire and ignite children's imaginations through the beauty of ballet, the magic of moving to music and the special world of storytelling. This unique program not only offers pre-school children the best introduction to sound ballet technique based on the principles of the Royal Academy of Dance (RAD) it also stimulates their imagination and enhances their experience of stories through kinesthetic movement.

The 8 Aims of the ballet program

- To nurture the imagination through ballet & drama
- To develop body awareness in relation to self and others
- To explore the joy of dance and drama
- To develop overall fitness
- To enhance the individuals creativity
- To build self-confidence

- To discover and explore individuality and self expression
- To learn the basic language of ballet

SPECIFICS

Length: 40 mins **Age:** 2.5 – 3.5 year olds

Length: 40 mins **Age:** 3.5 – 4.5 year olds

Students: Maximum of 11 children per class

Instruction: 1 Teacher

PRE LESSON SET UP CHECKLIST - VENUE

Room/Space - Clear the space. Remove anything that's hazardous. Sweep if necessary.

Toilets - Check lights are on and there's paper.

Lighting - Turn on all lights.

Heating/Cooling - Assess temperature and adjust climate. If hot, ensure all fans are on.

If cold, turn on all heaters so the environment is warm prior to children and parents arriving.

Chairs for parents - Set up in waiting room or up the back of the studio.

Pull-up banner - Place banner either outside where people can see it or, if windy inside.

Place weights on banner.

BALLET LESSON SET UP CHECKLIST – CLASS

LIST

- Roll Sheet/Clipboard
- Music
- Scarves
- Wands
- Cushions
- Mats
- Trees
- Flower Balls
- Stickers

DANCE FLOOR LAYOUT

I used mats to mark out spacing and places on the floor for children to stand in lines. These mats were like large computer mouse mats and adhered well to the floor and had a pretty pattern. They were extremely successful and very useful for organizing and arranging the children. I also used two stools and trees to mark the corners of the room to teach children about stagecraft, again very useful and successful.

POST LESSON PACK UP CHECKLIST

- Toilet lights off and locked
- Room back as it was
- Curtains closed
- Heaters off
- Fans/cooling off
- Props packed up
- Kitchenette tidied and wiped down
- Lights off
- Security alarm on

OUTCOMES OF THE PRESCHOOL BALLET PROGRAM

Children will learn:

- Full body stretches
- Balletic runs on demi-pointe
- Classical ballet walks
- Sways and spins with scarves
- Introduction to plies
- Pointing and flexing feet with elongated backs and arms
- Soft, slow spins
- Marching with opposite arms
- Improvisation
- Basic points and tendus and sautés
- Balance and core strength
- Body Isolation
- Mime and ballet demi - character
- Gallops
- Partner work
- Basic prop use
- Identifying different body parts
- An understanding of French ballet language for certain steps
- How to take directions
- Understanding of how their own bodies move within the space
- How to listen to instructions/descriptions
- The experience of dancing to music freely
- Moving to the timing and counting of the music
- Moving in the space with and around others
- How to co-ordinate and arrange their physical self
- To use their imagination and create ideas in their minds eye

- About 'Pretend' – an early form of mime and drama
- To respond and react to fellow children
- Watch and integrate in a group of peers
- How to stand out and in front of a group – early performance training

TEACHING CHILDREN BALLET/DANCE/DRAMA/ PERFORMANCE

- **EXPLAIN** - Explain everything you are doing, they will learn by absorbing everything you do. They will watch and take in everything.

- **PRESENTER** - Imagine you're like a children's TV presenter – enhance and exaggerate, point things out.

- **IMAGINATION** - Delve into your own imagination and 'Paint A Picture' for the children.

- **SENSES** – Remind the children what you can see, feel, smell.

- **FACE** - Use big, strong facial expressions.

- **VOICE** - Use a strong animated voice that changes, ebbs and flows, soft and loud.

- **QUESTIONS** – Ask the children lots of questions eg.

    - What might we hear in the garden?

    - What might this animal sound like?

    - How might this food smell?

- **WAND** – When using a wand, use it to enhance and conduct.

BALLET GLOSSARY

I also included a ballet glossary to remind teachers of the meanings of steps. I explained the meaning and the derivation of plié, tendus, pique, jete, pirouette and more. This meant that they were refreshed with the ballet terms and would use the correct terminology with the children. It's important to not underestimate what children are capable of and what they can learn, they will grasp the French ballet terminology if they are taught it from a young age.

BALLET CORRECTIONS

It is essential to be correcting children even at this early stage. Most of the time you will be saying general corrections to the group when you are demonstrating, like "press those shoulders down", "stretch those feet", "graceful arms", "eyes up" etc. Certain children will need to be corrected individually if they seem to be doing something that could cause a problem to their training or body alignment.

Most Common Corrections To Note:

- **Demi pointe** – Make sure children understand that demi pointe is where the toe joints flex; demi pointe is NOT full point. Even if we use the colloquial term 'tippy toes' we actually mean demi pointe, so if a child is going too high they need to be corrected.

- **Rise in parallel before starting an exercise** – Make sure any rises in parallel, the ankles really stay together in the rise before they then move, it's important for the alignment of the whole leg.

- **Demi plié** – Knees need to be ideally bending over the alignment of the second toe. If a child is really rolling in or out, they need to have their first position brought in a bit so their knees are more aligned over the second toe. As a teacher don't demonstrate a first position that is too turned out, otherwise children will copy and overly turn out when they haven't built the strength or capacity to do this.

- **Sickled Feet** – As we are teaching children early on about good toes and naughty toes, if you see a really sickled foot, run over and correct it. It needs to be aligned into a straight lovely pointed foot.

- **Posture** – Remind them to be straight as if they're wearing a crown. Always remind them they are like a princess or a queen, with a lovely straight back. If a child has a very obvious 'C' shaped arching back, gently remind them when you're near them to just straighten up. Don't mention 'tummy' in too much, Mums may get funny about this and associate it with weight. Mainly focus on a straight posture and that should rectify the tummy.

- **Gentle & Lovely** – Say all corrections in a soft, gentle, nurturing and lovely way; don't be harsh, strict or judgmental.

BALLET PROGRAM CLASS STRUCTURE – 5 KEY SECTIONS
- Introduction
- Centre/Circle
- Corner
- Dances

- Finish

This is the basic ballet class structure. We are aiming to teach children very early on how a ballet class works and what is expected of them, keeping with a strong fairy theme. Not a 'story' as such but a fairy theme, which incorporates fairy themed settings and characters.

Required:

- Always open the class with the welcome introduction and ballet stretches.

- Complete approximately 2 – 3 exercises each week from Centre/Circle and Corner work so children are covering 5 – 8 exercises each week from these sections.

- Always complete 1 of the 'dances' this allows them to learn a longer amount of sequential movements and early choreography.

- Always finish off with the Free Movements Dance.

DEMONSTRATE/SHOW/EXPLAIN

At this young age children really are learning from all their senses, they will 'copy' and watch everything you do, they are also 'modeling' your behavior and actions. It is vital to demonstrate every exercise with properly executed technique. The children only see/experience ballet for 1 x 40 minute session per week with 6 days in between, this is why it's important to continue to demonstrate to them each and every week.

Teacher Handbook

The Information Manual was very focused on the actual class, ballet technique, the room setup, what the objectives are and what the children will achieve. Its sole purpose was about the classes. The Teacher Handbook is actually about the practicalities of working for you. What's expected, what's needed, what the standards are, how training works and how they'll be remunerated. It is the practical, business side of things. Use this as a guide when you develop your own handbook.

EXAMPLE

Teacher Handbook

TABLE OF CONTENTS

ABC DANCE SCHOOL Mission/Vision/AimValues
The Practical Guide
What to Wear
Classes
Marketing/Media
Training Session
Remuneration
Parents/Guardians/Carers
Please Provide Your Details
Dance and drama teacher full position description
ABC DANCE SCHOOL'S responsibilities to teachers
Final thoughts...

*Write your own mission, vision and aim for the overall business. Read these often as they keep you on track, on target and inspired!**

EXAMPLE

MISSION

"Our mission is to enhance children's imaginations, creativity and wellbeing through our innovative, inspiring and enriching teachers and programs."

VISION

"Our vision is to enrich the lives of children, to support them on their journey to become happy, positive and proactive people who will grow to live strong, healthy and imaginative lives."

AIM

"We aim to create a colourful, caring and nurturing environment which will positively impact on each and every one of the children who come to learn with us."

VALUES

Write your values down – what are the main values you have regarding teaching children?

The Practical Guide

TEACHING PRACTICALITIES

WHAT TO WEAR

It's important to project a lovely, polished image to parents and children. This also really encourages parents and guardians to take the time to appropriately dress their child for class. These early disciplines are very important.

It's also important to project the quality of dance as our style as opposed to sport. With attire I want to make sure what you wear has a 'dancey' feel as opposed to a 'sporty/gym'.

Top: Any white, pink or purple gripper top, ideally with a sleeve or cap sleeve.

*My teachers opted for a dark purple, cap-sleeved leotard.

Bottom: ¾ black opaque tights with dance/ballet wrap around skirt in pink, purple or black, or ¾ fitted gym pants in black or grey only. No colors.

Footwear: Ballet flats – leather, canvas i.e. sansha or something similar.

Hair: Ideally – Bun/French roll or up in an alligator clip. If this is impractical, neatly tied back in a low ponytail. If you have short, styled hair, absolutely fine.

CLASSES

Timetables: These will be sent via email. New ones will be emailed if there are any changes. New ones will also be emailed at the beginning of every term to outline any changes, indicate public holidays or any other important things to know.

Schedule: All classes run for 40minutes. There is a 5-minute gap between each class to allow for teachers to gather themselves for the next class or answer any urgent questions etc.

Roll sheets: You will receive complete roll sheets for each class via email, as it's the quickest way to allow for changes and updates. When children are enrolled they will be on your roll sheet. If a child has not been fully paid for, for the term they wont appear on the roll. For insurance reasons they cannot continue classes with you unless they've been paid for.

Carry out all duties: It's important not to enlist assistants or contractors underneath you unless discussed with us.

Holidays: It's important that any holiday dates or days where you will have to be away during school term, you inform us in the week before a new term begins. As all classes run to the school term, you get a two-week break between each term. You also get the full summer school holidays off, so any holidays that fall outside of this need to be noted.

Sick: If you are feeling very unwell it is ideal you give us a full 24hours notice so we are able to email/sms parents. In some cases, you may need to inform parents, this will be discussed.

Probationary Period: Probation is the entirety of one full term of teaching; at the end of the term it is assessed and discussed as to whether the classes/location is viable to continue and whether contracts will be continued.

Free Trial Class: Once per year in the first week of the first term we run a promotion where there are classes classified as 'trial classes' for NEW students only. This happens once in a whole year. These 'trial classes' only run for ½ an hour as opposed to the usual 40minutes. This invites new people from the community to experience the programs and meet you.

Demonstration Day: The very last class in the last week of every term is 'Demo Day' and children are to come looking their best in their class uniform. Parents will be sent a note/email and they are invited to come and watch their children. In the last 10 minutes of the 'Demo Day' we ask teachers to take some photos for marketing purposes. When you announce this, some parents will want to remove their children from the class for the last 10 minutes, this is perfectly fine. Written permission must be given for children to have their photos taken.

Venues: The venues you are teaching at will all be clearly explained via email, listed on the website and discussed with you. All keys will be arranged the week before or in the week you commence teaching. It is your responsibility to manage keys; you will also be given contact details for the venues if any problems should arise.

Feedback on venues is also paramount, if you or parents and children are finding certain venues are raising issues, we will all work together to find a better one.

Other Locations: If you know of another location/suburb near you that would also be great for classes, let us know and we can organize everything to get up and running there!

Insurance: You are completely covered by our public liability insurance for every venue you work in. If you want to take out your own that's completely up to you but it is not necessary. If you are interested to take out your own we can advise you of who we use.

Working with Children Certificate (Australia): Be sure to give us a copy of a current certificate called the 'Certificate for Self Employed People'.

Medical conditions: Be sure to tell us of any medical condition, which may affect your work performance.

Termination – As per the Contract of Employment

MARKETING/MEDIA

Marketing Activity: All marketing, advertising, events, promotions and partnerships are generated from us. If you have some wonderful ideas on how to communicate with the community, parents and children we are all in favor of that and welcome ideas!!

Media: From time to time, if there's interest from a journalist, you may be required to have a photo shoot with a few children. If this is something you are not in a position to do, please let us know. If this opportunity arose, I would ask that you recommend a child and parent from your class that would seem to be willing to do something like this, so I can best arrange this type of opportunity. Again written and signed permission from the parents is required for this to happen.

Websites: Our websites are mainly there to inform people of what we do. It would be lovely for you to read the websites to be across the objectives etc. Information for teachers will always be emailed or posted directly to you.

Social Media: It would be great to encourage parents to 'like' us or 'follow' us on our Facebook page.

TRAINING SESSION

Times: Training session days are 9.30AM – 4.30PM with a 1-hour break for lunch where we'll go to a café, to get away from the workspace.

What to bring: Yourself, your ideas, water, snacks, and comfortable clothes to move in.

Provided: Program guides, props, notepad, pen, and music.

Payment: Training is paid. This is paid at the end of Term 1 (probationary period), regardless of whether you continue working with us. As you can appreciate, we need to do this to avoid the unlikely incident of people receiving full training, receiving payment for it and then leaving.

REMUNERATION

ABN: You are required to provide us with your full name and ABN (Australia) or equivalent.

Invoice: You will be required to invoice us on the Friday at the end of each 2 week period as outlined in the contract. A tax invoice template is attached to this document as a guide, feel free to use it.

Administration at half rate: If there are a few administrative tasks that need to be carried out by you from time to time, outline these and invoice at ½ your hourly rate.

PARENTS/GUARDIANS/CARERS

Payments: Under no circumstances do you need to accept or discuss any aspect of payments with parents. Any payment inquiries or issues need to be directed straight back to us. Parents may attempt to give you cash or bank deposits, it's important not to take them.

Notes/Surveys/Reminders: From time to time you will be given notes to hand out to parents.

Collection/Suggestion Box: If we decided it's useful we may provide you with a medium sized box, a bit like an election day voting collection box (not that big). It can stand in the studio where the parents sit and this way they can write a suggestion down, rather than discussing it with you. This may also be used for surveys or forms etc.

Uniform: Parents may ask you what their child should wear to class. All of these details are on the website. Depending on what class the child is in the uniform is listed.

Communication from parents: We have a 'zero tolerance policy on disrespect', if parents are disrespectful please direct any issues to us and we will deal directly with parents.

PLEASE PROVIDE PRIOR TO TRAINING SESSION:

To ensure everything runs smoothly, please provide the following before the training session.

- Please Provide Your: (Australia)

- ABN via Email
- Bank account details for direct deposit via Email
- 'Certificate for Self-Employed People in a Child Related Environment'
- Short Bio and head shot for website via Email
- Any medical issues we need to be aware of via Email
- Next of kin name and phone number via Email
- Signed and initialed contract via Post
- Please Email to: abcdanceschool@..............

Dance teacher full position description

Once you've come on board its good to be clear about what is expected.

Your responsibilities are in relation to:

Class Structure | You are required to:

- Teach ABC program to children. The classes are 40 minutes in length and are structured according to the Program.

- Teach the Program according to the 'Teachers Dance Instruction Guide' so that there is consistency and quality control for parents and children.

- Arrive at the venue ten minutes (minimum) prior to class starting in time to open, set up the props and make the space tidy for the arrival of children and parents.

Customer Service

You are required to:

- Foster, build and maintain positive relationships with children by demonstrating patience, kindness and a nurturing attitude.

- Build and maintain respectful and positive relationships with parents.

- Exhibit excellent communication and customer service skills and have the ability to listen to children and parents and respond to their needs accordingly and direct inquiries related to fees or complaints to us.

Your Input | You are required to:

- Maintain positive working relationships with the Program Director and be willing to accept constructive feedback and participate in ongoing training and development offered by us.

- Assist in the collection of Parent Feedback in the form of surveys or anecdotally regarding the programs to enable us to work on continuous improvement of service delivery for you, parents and children.

- Communicate regularly via email with the Program Director regarding any questions, issues or clarifications within the scope of the work.

- Provide all services to the best of your ability and represent us at all times in a professional and reputable manner.

ABC's Responsibilities to Teachers

Code of Conduct

- You will be treated with respect at all times.

- We will support and assist you to be the best Teacher you can possibly be.

- We will support and nurture your teaching with training discussion, feedback, and meetings.

- We will operate in a professional and ethical manner at all times.

Employment/Remuneration

- Any changes to employment conditions will be discussed with you.

- You will be paid the agreed amount plus superannuation.

- ABC can terminate the 'Independent Contractor's Service Agreement' with the Teacher with 2 weeks notice.

Classes/Training/Equipment

- Venues - We will inform you of venue changes.

- Programs – You will be provided with all training materials at no expense to you.

- Props - You will be provided with all props needed to carry out classes at no cost to you.

In Summary...

- Aim for excellent over competent teachers

- Show respect, listen and acknowledge teachers

- Have organised training days and face to face meetings

- Provide manuals, information and materials

- Hire for enthusiasm, commitment and love of children not just CV credentials

- Maintain high standards and expectations of people

CHAPTER 5

CUSTOMER RELATIONSHIPS AND COMMUNICATION SKILLS

Our dance studios are made up of many people. Think of all the groups: teachers, students, parents, guest teachers, our family, our accountant/bookkeeper and other technical people and government people we have to deal with. Plus we mustn't forget cleaners, costume makers and photographers. The list just goes on and on!

As teachers and studio owners we often find ourselves with two roles or 'hats' - Hat 1 Dance Teacher, Hat 2 Studio Director or vice versa. The challenge arises in the mechanics of how these roles get played out in the day-to-day operations of running your studio. More often than not it is this one challenge that sits at the forefront of the difficulties in relationships - predominantly between yourself and parents and sometimes other teachers.

What I've Observed

I've observed and analysed over the years how studios are run plus I've had my own experience sitting on both sides of the fence as both a teacher and a studio director.

The Ideal - **I've come to the conclusion that the most effective and streamlined system is this:**

- **A Studio Director** - This person runs the place, runs a tight ship, on top of accounts - they are the "business person" and they deal with all parental demands.

- **Head/Principal Teacher** - Focuses solely on teaching, choreography, exams, comps, classes, student development, programming, other teachers and so on.

Now, in this situation, the studio director may own the business and employ the teachers or the head dance teacher owns the business and employs the studio director. Either way can work.

The Challenge

Most new and even long running established schools don't have the resources to have a studio director. So they end up delivering both roles themselves. What they love is the teaching, creating, student development etc and where the hiccups arise is in trying to also struggle with the time it takes 'running a business'. I've seen this so many times.

The Remedy?

If you're reading this and you already employ a person/ family member/co-founder who does the Studio Director role, great! If not these are some options:

1. **Solid Plan To Get Someone on Board** - Organising a solid business/financial plan over the next 18 months to 3 years to bring in enough students to generate the monetary resources required to be able to get someone on-board to do this role, even part time, is a good answer to the problem.

2. **Boundary Setting** - This is about deciding when you are and aren›t available to parents and other people - this 100% has to happen and can happen fairly quickly when implemented correctly.

3. **Communication & Leadership** - As the head teacher/Principal you can work on a range of skills that make you more powerful and influential as the school grows.

I have seen this so many times in dance studios and sadly when it is not 'sorted out' it can grind away at the person trying to juggle the 2 Hats as well as all the other roles that make up those two hats!

I have also seen some streamlined, effective tight ship studios where these challenges have been 'got on top of' and the results are very good and a lot less stressful.

Sometimes we can become defeatist and think it's too hard to shift so we stay plodding along. My message to you is this - it takes small steps at first, yes, it can seem slow and no it won't change over night but yes it can change in time.

One of the most important but also most dynamic and at times challenging and even difficult groups to deal with is the parents. As dance studio directors and teachers we need the parents as much as they need us. The complicated part is that we are in the type of business where the 'end user' or customer who uses our services is more than one person – the parent (who pays) and the student (who attends).

Think about a hair salon, the end user is Jenny who comes in to have her hair cut and coloured. One person: she comes in, she experiences the service and then she pays and leaves. With dance studios, performing arts studios or any other 'children's activities' services the person who pays the bill is a different person to the one who experiences the service. This means that we have to be on our toes when it comes to relating to this group effectively. It's a weigh up between stating our authority and being in charge and also being friendly, warm and approachable.

So, let's break this down.

OUR BEHAVIOUR TOWARDS PARENTS (Too friendly)

- Friendly all the time
- Giving a lot of time before or after class
- Allowing parents to converse at the studio about 'issues' they have
- Let them off paying fees on time
- Give in to all their requests
- Have the mantra 'the customer is always right'

PARENTS REACTION TO THIS BEHAVIOUR

- They can perceive you as weak
- They can sometimes take advantage of your time

- Can assume their own 'power position' in front of other parents and you

- Think they can just change the rules

- Don't take you or the studio seriously enough

- They can become unreasonable and disrespect your authority

OUR BEHAVIOUR TOWARDS PARENTS (Too strict)

- Strict and terse in manner

- Get a sense of power from being short and cold with people

- Don't talk, see or communicate with the parents much

- Don't smile much and exercise rigid body language

PARENTS REACTION TO THIS BEHAVIOUR

- They can think you're mean and unfriendly

- They can wonder why they're paying you and not another studio

- They may disrespect and gossip about you behind your back which can create a tense studio culture

- They may not want to continue sending their child to your studio

What I have sometimes seen with people I work with in the past is that sometimes teachers felt they needed to state their authority but they didn't know how to do it. Often when people don't know how to effectively state their authority they go for the hard, closed, cold approach. This can lead to alienation from parents and even a bad reputation for you and your studio.

Even if a teacher is really nice to the students, if they are unfriendly or unpleasant to parents this method wont work - especially in this day and age.

So, what's the answer?

As studio owners, dance directors and dance teachers we are also businesswomen and men and we need to have the intention and expectation of generating respect, a sense of leadership and the power of influence so the role we are in is honoured by those around us.

There are 3 powerful qualities we need to acquire:
- Credibility
- Conviction
- Confidence

1. CREDIBILITY - Dictionary Definition: The quality of being trusted and believed in.

When a person comes across as credible, people take notice. People listen, look up to and respect that the person in question is on top of their game.

How do we come across as more credible?

There are certain things we can do to increase our credibility. Often our own background, experience and skillset tell us theoretically we are credible however our rate of credibility in the eyes of others needs to be of focus.

Building Credibility in Practical Terms

Be Sophisticated – People who are sophisticated come across as mature and in control and more credible.

Language – Credible language is objective, certain, non-emotional, professional and business-like. It includes phrases like:

- "I'm not in a position to..."
- "This type of conversation needs to happen at X time..."
- "We don't have these kinds of conversations at this studio."
- "I appreciate what you're saying however we're not in a position to..."
- "I appreciate where you're coming from however, I'm not at liberty to..."
- "There's some confusion here."

You can still be friendly, you can still smile but the words you use and the tone you use is certain, strong and matter-of-fact. It is also important to face the person and not turn away as this looks as though you are trying to avoid saying whatever it is you need to say.

Impressions - Wear a stylish suit jacket once per week, and then slowly increase it.

(This acts as an anchor)

Approach when on the phone:

- Wear a suit jacket
- Wear heels (if heels make you feel strong)

- Stand up – this makes your voice/tone more powerful

2. CONVICTION - Dictionary Definition - a fixed or firm belief:

People who have strong conviction know what they do and don't want. What they do and don't value and what they do and don't believe. The stronger you are in your own thoughts and beliefs the more conviction you will have.

In order to get stronger and have more conviction we have to work on our knowledge, decision-making skills and mode of operation.

How can we develop stronger conviction?

There is a fair amount of 'inner work' and questioning that needs to be done to develop conviction but a good start is to answer these questions:

QUESTIONS (write down your answers)
- Am I assertive?
- Am I good at making decisions?
- Am I a planned and organized person?
- Am I sure of myself?
- Do I trust others?
- Am I open to change?
- How do I want my life to look?
- Am I idealistic, realistic, pessimistic or optimistic?

QUESTIONS - List at least 10 responses for each
- What are my non-negotiables?
- What do I disapprove of?
- What makes me angry?

- What character traits in others do I believe are good?
- How do I expect others to treat me?
- What are my expectations of others?
- What is my work ethic?
- What strong character traits do I have?
- Why am I in business?

3. CONFIDENCE – Dictionary Definition – belief in one-self and one's powers or abilities: self-confidence

Shift your focus

To be confident we need to focus on the 'good stuff' we need to consistently see what we are good at, what we excel at and what makes us feel good. We need to not dip into seeing negatives. When we know more about our strengths, wins, skills and abilities we have more confidence.

Some confidence building questions:

List at least 5 answers to each question

- What are my best qualities?
- What am I really good at?
- What wins have I had in my life?
- What moments in my life made me feel amazing and filled me up?
- Who in my life supports me and makes me feel good?
- What inspires me?
- How do I pamper myself and rejuvenate so I feel good?
- Who do I look up to?

How to outwardly look confident when we're still inwardly working on being more confident

- Walk tall – good, strong posture makes us look and feel more confident

- Balanced posture – Ensure your weight is even and you're not slouched or slumped on one side, don't cross your feet or sink into your hip when you're presenting or talking to people face to face

- Strong handshake – when meeting someone have a firm handshake

- Don't fiddle/fidget – Be solid and strong and don't fiddle with things or fidget eg. biting nails, biting pens, playing with fingers, hair etc.

- Upbeat strong voice – Aim to have a voice that has a level of 'command' to it. If your voice is positive and upbeat (not too high in tone) you come across as enthusiastic rather than downbeat, which can be seen as oppressive or moody, (less powerful).

- Attire – Aim to wear more commanding outfits eg. Stronger more fitted outfits, fashionable suit jackets, darker colors, and fewer accessories. The more fitted, strong and angular your clothes are the stronger you appear.

- Stay out of drama – Confident people don't get dramatic/over the top or exaggerate facts because they know who they are, what they want and what they stand for. People who get caught up in drama operate on a different level with low-level tactics for achieving power and confidence.

Dealing with "Difficult" Parents or People at the School

Difficult people are everywhere and they will always be around us. We have to be quick at spotting this type of person so we know our mechanism for dealing with them. Difficult people often have little power or control in their own personal circumstances or history and so they are out to get power whenever they can.

These people often use an overt form of power which can be anything from cursing, yelling, scowling and intimidating to persecuting, judging, comparing and so on. It also needs to be remembered that difficult people can also be non-overt in the form of sleazy, manipulative, passive-aggressive, whiney or upset. This form is generally easier to deal with on a day-to-day level but ultimately can be very destructive. Both kinds of people/character traits are after one thing – power.

People & Power

People who want things their way exercise their power to get what they want. Most people have done this to get what they want at some point in their lives and we all do it from time to time without realizing it. The sooner you work out who has the power in any given situation the quicker you can change it around.

The emotional, defensive, rude, inappropriate person always holds the power while the other person is 'taking the bait' this means so long as person 1 throws forward their bait and person 2 catches it and responds, justifies and defends their position the longer person 1 will hold the power.

How to move into the power position to claim authority over the situation

1. A separation from emotion, justification, defense or drama always cools the heat of the conversation.

2. Analogy – difficult person is the fire, other person defends and justifies, this breathes more oxygen into the difficult person's fire (giving them more power). As long as the less powerful person in the situation continues to buy into the difficult person's persecution the longer the difficult person will have their fire enhanced and it will grow and their power position may win over the other person.

3. Cool Off – We literally have to cool off. We have to not allow their heat to growbigger. The way to cool off is to only ever call on the person's behavior not the person, eg: Say in a cool, calm voice something like:

   - "The tone you are using is inappropriate"
   - "I wont be continuing this conversation while I'm being spoken to in this manner"
   - "I'm a business person and I don't have people speak to me like this"
   - "Mrs Jones, you are (name the behavior) yelling/ being offensive/name calling and I don't have conversations with people who are behaving like this so I wont be able to continue this conversation until that behavior's stopped."

4. Don't Do (personal)

   - "Mrs Jones, you're a really rude person."
   - "You're a gossip."

- "You're talking crap."
- "You're upsetting me."

5. Removing personal language, creating separation from emotion and calling people on their behavior are good tools to use to get your own power back.

6. Handing Over Decisions/Changes/Responsibility

Another tool people can use is to hand over decisions/ responsibility to an external source that is impersonal and can't be argued with eg

- "My accountant says..."
- "My business advisor says..."
- "The legalities are..."
- "The insurance situation is..."
- "The dance industry body says..."

This implies an official secondary power. A person questioning you on the issue at hand has nowhere to go on this because you have removed yourself as the authority and have placed it into the hands of an official/legal body. This quickly shuts down people who are challenging things.

Email Communication

When you run a studio the amount of emails you send will be huge and will often contain similar information, updates, instructions, attachments and details. One way to make this really simple and streamlined is to have stock standard emails written with the bulk of the content all the same. Then, all you have to do is amend the dates/names etc.

The great thing about standardized emails too is that you can have a timeline of when to send them out so no one ever misses out on receiving information from you.

Emails to Parents

The language when dealing with parents needs to be friendly but firm, upbeat but assertive and above all clear and concise. I highly recommend ensuring all emails contain the following key aspects:

- Dot points – when you have more than several points, use a dot point list rather than blocks of text.
- Bold the title then the information – write the main point in bold then the content unbold.
- Repeat, repeat, repeat – never be concerned to say too many important things again and again. People are really busy, it's better to say the same important information over and over again in a few emails over a few weeks than only say it once and people miss it.
- Short and to the point – Aim to keep emails short and sharp, lots of divisions of text with sub headlines in bold and underlined, dot points and no rambling on.
- Opening – Always be friendly, upbeat and nice – a hello, a welcome, exclamation marks and smiley faces.
- Closing – Sign off in a friendly manner, upbeat and enthusiastic.
- Email tone – the 'voice' that comes across in the emails needs to be friendly but also a little bit 'headmistress' what I mean by that is, you need to have an element of 'Mary Poppins' no nonsense to the email, this way you will come across as organized and as

if your business is run like a tight ship. People feel secure when things are highly organized and you have a good sense of leadership.

EMAIL TEMPLATE EXAMPLES

I developed several stock standard emails that I could send when that time of year rolled around again and below I have included these emails for you to give you an idea of the voice, layout and length. Use these as a guide when you're constructing your own emails.

TRIAL CLASS EMAIL

When to send: 1 Day prior to the Trial

Subject: Only 24hrs till the Ballet Class Trial!

Hello! :)

We look forward to welcoming you and your little ballerina along tomorrow afternoon for class with Miss X for the ABC Ballet Class Trial Lesson :)

**Please let me know if you can't come along so I can let another little ballerina have your spot.

You Are Registered for:

Time: 4.15PM - 4.55PM

Venue: X Recreation Centre corner of Brown Rd and Fifty Rd (Blue Building)

Date: Tomorrow - Tuesday Feb 4th

Teacher: Miss Betty Brown

What to Wear: Something fitted that your daughter can move in. Bare feet or grip socks (Just for this first class). Hair pulled back off face in a ponytail or a bun. Please no jiffies, big skirts, dresses.

Enrolment: If after the class you would like to enrol your daughter please type in the form attached to this email and email it back to me :)

Miss Betty Brown does not accept payments in person. If you would like to do the enrolment over the phone with me that's fine, please reply to this email and let me know the best number to call you on.

Thank You so much and we hope you enjoy the Trial,

Emma!

FIRST EMAIL AFTER ENROLLMENT

When to Send: Before Week 1

Subject Line: Welcome to ABC Ballet

Hello & Welcome to ABC Ballet for Pre-schoolers!

As you and your daughter are now valued members of ABC Ballet we welcome you along every week to class and we hope your daughter learns and develops as well as has lots of fun with her ballet friends and Miss Betty :)

Details Recap - (10 Week Term)

Start Date: Tuesday 29th April - Tuesday 1st July

End Date: Demonstration Day/Certificates: Tues 1st July

Venue: Nelson Region Hall cnr Smith St, Madison

Tutu if you are new: To pick up on your first day - tomorrow!

Viewing Class: Feel free to view the first 2-3 classes so your daughter feels comfortable. As she gains confidence we do advise you to step into the foyer or wait somewhere on the premises or in the car. This confidence usually happens by about week 3-4.

Allowing your daughter to attend class on her own just with the other students and Miss Betty is wonderful for her own self-confidence & development. This also keeps the work for Demonstration Day a surprise for you!

Shoes/Tights - We require you to purchase some ballet shoes for your new ballerina so she is not only safe and comfortable but also feels the part of a ballet dancer in these early years of learning :)

Tights - We encourage you to purchase ballet tights for your child but they are not compulsory. As an alternative, little white/flesh/pink socks (no patterns) can be worn in shoes.

We recommend **ABC Dance Shop: 15 Brown St, Perth Contact: Sally** 0401 111 XXX

**Please mention you are doing classes at ABC Ballet as Sally fits most of the girls and knows what they wear :)

We thank you so much for enrolling your daughter and investing in her dance & drama development :)

EMAIL TO ENCOURAGE PARENTS TO SIT OUTSIDE

When to send: Week 3 of Term

Subject: Confidence & Ballet Principles

Hello,

Just a quick little email to say as the girls are building their confidence and bonding with Miss Betty we often do recommend from about week 4 (next week) Mums & Dads can have the opportunity to let their daughter attend ballet by herself for her full development :)

It is great for them to see that ballet lessons become a focus between the other students and the teacher, this is so good for their self-esteem, self-confidence and personal pride.

Distractions - For most students this 40 mins is their only time in a ballet class of this nature in the week, therefore we really need to decrease distractions. If mums & dads and siblings can wait outside or in the outer section of the hall we would really appreciate this.

Thank you for your understanding and interest in what's best for the students :)

Emma & teacher

EMAIL FOR DEMONSTRATION DAY AND RE-ENROLLMENT

When to send: The Saturday before or the Monday of the Week of Demo Day

Subject: Demonstration Day & Re-Enrollment Updates

Hello!

Wow! We can't believe it's Demonstration Day this week!

Demonstration Day Important Notes:

Please be at class 5-10mins before your class time so your daughter can go to the bathroom before she starts class.

Please have her hair nice and neatly pulled back into a ballet bun or ponytail.

Ballet tights and ballet shoes are to be worn.

Feel free to take as many photos/videos at Demo Day as you like - this is your opportunity to really capture what she's learnt this Term :)

Feel free to send some pics through to me! I'd love to see the girls and share a few on our Facebook page :)

Friends & Family - this is your opportunity to have friends and family come along.

Priority Re-Enrolment:

You can jump the queue and have the wonderful opportunity to re-enrol your ballerina back into ballet for Term 4 at the same class time before anyone else!!

TO DO:

Reply to this email: If you are using the same credit card as last term- simply reply to this email saying

"Yes, I want to re-enrol my daughter in the same class at the same time. Yes, Please charge the same Credit Card as last time."

OR

Fill in New Credit Card Form Attached: If you want to use a different card simply fill in the details in the form attached.

OR

I Can Call You: If you want to change classes, have a new credit card etc – Simply let me know the best number to call you on and I can process your details over the phone.

We look forward to welcoming you and your ballerina back to ballet for Term 4.

EMAIL FOR BALLET FINAL UPDATE FOR THE TERM OR YEAR

When to Send: Saturday after Demonstration Day

Subject: Thank You for a Wonderful Term OR Thank You for a Wonderful Year

Hello All Current Members :)

Thank you so so much for a fabulous final term at ABC Ballet! We were thrilled and delighted to have you at ABC Ballet, I hope you had a lovely time at Demonstration Day and if you have any photos to send through, feel free to do that anytime :)

Holiday Cheer! We really wish you a lovely break with your family and friends over Christmas and hope that you get some quality time with your loved ones. New Year is also a fantastic time to think about the year ahead and get excited about what may be in store :)

20XX Enrolment Info: For little ballerinas who would like to continue back with us next year we will be sending a priority email out to you, our current members on Monday January 6th. This gives you 1 week to jump in and enrol before we open up spots to keen new ballerinas.

Note: If you already know you want to return, reply to this email and let me know, then I can just finalise the enrolment fee with you in the first week of January.

Testimonial: Did you enjoy your time with ABC Ballet this year? Did your little one enjoy learning from Miss Prue or Miss Betty? I would be so, so grateful if you had a few mins to write a quick couple of sentences about your experience with us. This helps other mums and dads decide where to send their little ballerina :) Simply reply to this email and let me know your thoughts :) Thank You for that.

I look forward to spending time with friends and family and heading up to the Blue Mountains and Central Coast where I have family and friends. It will be nice to get out of the city for a bit :)

Many thanks and best wishes, Emma :)

EMAIL FOR NEW YEAR ENROLMENTS

When to send: The week before enrolments 'officially' open

Subject: Hello & Happy New Year!

Hello Everyone!

We hope you had a wonderful Christmas and a bright and cheerful New Year with lots of exciting things coming up in 2014!

ABC Ballet is now taking enrolments for all current members :) You have 1 week where enrolments are exclusively offered to current members :) Next week enrolments will be open to the general public.

NOTE:

If you would like to re-enrol you daughter into the same class using the same credit card, please hit 'reply' to this email and write:

Yes, I would like to re-enrol my daughter into the same class using the same credit card.

If you need to purchase a new Tutu for the reduced rate of $25 please also write:

I also need a new Tutu for my daughter in size (write size)

20XX Price Guide:

Ballet Term Fees for 10 Ballet Classes = $160.00

X LOCATION Dates: Tuesdays

Term Starts: Tues 4th Feb

Term Ends: Tues 8th April

X LOCATION Dates: Thursdays

Term Starts: Thurs 6th Feb

Term Ends: Thurs 10th April

Miss Betty & Miss Prue look forward to working with your daughter again in 20XX and seeing her grow and develop in dance.

Look forward to hearing from you, Thanks, Emma :)

In Summary...

- Customer communication, connection and relationship building is key

- Leadership will give you gravitas and strength an respect

- Credibility, conviction and confidence will generate respect from parents

- Be strong, solid and sophisticated but never personal, rude or short

- Don't get caught up in the Drama Triangle – ever.

- Keep up communication via emails, newsletters, social media

- Develop lots of touch points to keep people 'in the loop'.

CHAPTER 6

PRICING, PAYMENT AND PROFIT

PRICING WILL ALWAYS BE A CHALLENGE IN A SMALL BUSINESS. You can spend hours and hours looking at what competitors are doing and wonder whether you should go cheaper or a little more expensive.

It's All About Value

At the end of the day you have to look at the value in your business, your offering, your product and the outcome for your customers. When it comes down to it, what people want is outcomes so the question is, what will they get in the end after all is said and done? For example if you're a personal trainer the "value" is in whether by following your steps your program and your philosophy, the person will be fit, slim (or desired weight), healthy and happy. The price charged is based on the value of that. The more you can show that following your way will give the person what they want the more you can charge.

In the dance industry we place our value on our students' learning, creative development, technical development and so much more. You have to gauge where you believe your classes fit within a range of classes on offer in the market. When I was running my ballet school I had developed a unique program which took time and lots of thought to create. I worked out that compared to other dance classes for preschoolers there was a lot of value in my classes.

Through my program children would learn:

- Ballet technique at the preschool level
- Ballet terminology
- How to use props
- Basic drama techniques
- Story structure
- How to follow a structured week to week program
- Learning choreography to music
- Listening to music
- How to behave in a group and solo
- How to listen and take directions from a teacher
- Posture and balance
- Spatial awareness
- Learning how to behave appropriately in class
- Respect for others
- Performing in front of an audience
- The importance of being dressed properly in ballet attire for each class

I worked out that what I created was well thought out, well crafted and I expected a certain level of commitment from students, parents and teachers. In return they received a lot of value and I charged a premium price for classes. Parents and teachers appreciated and valued the fact that it was a totally unique program, well structured, beautiful to watch and full of solid learning about ballet and music in a fun and age-appropriate framework.

Work out what it is that your students are getting from your classes and base your value on that and not on what the dance school down the road is charging.

Low Price Point

Some classes you run may be very basic, not a thought out structure, no performances or high expectations. Children basically come for a bit of "fun". I would be pricing these classes at a lower level and paying teacher's less than I would for more serious classes.

Standard Price Point

Classes at this level are priced at a mid-range, standard price point. The teacher has a solid amount of experience, the parents have a certain level of expectation and the students are expected to attend class presenting themselves in a neat and tidy way. A lot of dance schools are at this level. The classes are not part of a unique program and this is a perfectly OK place to be operating, however these types of classes will never rise up to a premium market level because they won't be recognized as offering extra value. They will be seen as 'quite good'. The aim (if you are ambitious) is to move from this level to premium and to do this you have to offer more value than the average class.

Premium Price Point

This level of class has the following criteria:

- An experienced mature teacher who is passionate about young children's development

- A limit on class sizes

- Good quality venue

- Attractive quality props that are kept to a high standard

- A uniform that is worn to each class (and can be included in term fees)

- A structured program with clearly stated objectives

- Demonstrated acknowledgement of work e.g. certificate presentation, recitals, ribbon on completion of terms/ years

- A performance/recital/concert/demonstration day

- Strong unique brand that differentiates this group of classes

- Market leader in this area

- Superior customer service and relationship building with parents

- An expectation from you that teachers, parents and students maintain a required level of commitment

- A strong personal standard of dance

- Teachers often trained in one of the recognized, registered dance methods

My focus is on getting you from wherever you are now to a premium level. When you're operating at a premium level certain things start to shift:

- Classes become more profitable
- "Premium" clients become your customers
- None or minimal chasing of fees
- You become more talked about and known as being premium
- Children behave better overall
- Teachers are more loyal
- You feel fantastic about what you do and offer and that it is at the best standard you can possibly reach
- Most parents will pay term fees up front without questions

What to charge:

If you believe that everything we have discussed is what you already have in place, fantastic! Next, I want you to find out the highest priced classes in your area and gradually increase your prices to match them. The best time for price increases is at the start of a new year.

Too many people in the performing arts industry under-sell, underprice and undervalue themselves, their skill and their dedication. This does not benefit anyone in the dance industry in fact it's quite the opposite – it can be damaging to the viability of people's businesses and can sadly see people go out of business.

You may find some parents leave your studio when your prices increase. That's OK, they are now not the right 'match' for you and your value level anymore. Everyone else who is new to your studio and is happy to pay the new price is a better match customer.

If you want to make the shift from where you are now to premium, map out what you need to do to get to the premium level:

PREMIUM MODEL

A Personal Example:

We were operating in the regional towns of southern Perth, Western Australia. Our model looked like this: These prices were in 2012 – 2014 in $AUD.

1. $160 for 10 lessons, $30 for mandatory class tutu included in enrolment

2. Total: $190 for first term fees and $160 for subsequent terms

3. This was significantly above other schools offering preschool classes in the same geographic area

4. We never accepted payment plans of any type

5. All our fees were paid upfront for the full term before the term started - no lingering unpaid accounts

6. We never had any complaints about price or about paying up front

7. We were never challenged on competitor's rates

8. We had no unpaid fees

You can achieve this by assessing your offering and then increasing your value and price.

How to take payments: (Australia)

We experimented with a number of payment methods from EFT, Cash, Cheque, PayPal and iPad bank APP.

Without a doubt the easiest, quickest and best way for us was by using our bank's credit card payment APP for ipad. It was so simple, so quick and we never made one error! It also offered an instant receipt to be sent to the parent's email. The only downside was the relatively high but comparable fees to PayPal and bank merchant services.

My Suggestions (A Personal Guide Only):

- I never had teachers taking payments from parents. All payments were organized directly through me.

- Cash can be problematic. It doesn't give a professional image to parents. You want to show them and "teach" them that you operate like a proper professional business. This increases the level of respect for you and your business.

- PayPal - unless you have a professional system a PayPal button on your website can cause 'class hijacking" where classes are overfilled without you knowing it because people have enrolled and paid via your website and you haven't had time to check on each enrollment as it comes in. This can lead to tension or dissatisfaction from parents. You want to be in control of your business as much as possible.

- You may be already using a sophisticated payment system designed just for your website or you've found a great studio payments software program. If so, that's great! If you are just starting out though, one of the more old fashioned ways will be what you are using and in the beginning, to lower the stress, I would consider the credit card payment APP for ipad that your bank offers.

Payments Upfront:

Your aim when running a dance school is to teach the parents how you work and what you expect from them and how you want to be treated. When you set clear ground rules with parents most of them will follow, accept, understand and oblige.

This is so important as it generates respect and once you have respect you are treated well and once you're treated well you can run a solid, flourishing and wonderful business.

Perfect Paying Parent Model

We want our parents to be happy and we want them to pay, "in full, on time, every time."

The way to do this:

- Give parents plenty of warning about upcoming enrolments and payments

- Give current students priority – this is a way of showing respect for the loyalty of your current students

- Maintain the same level of service and value throughout the whole term so that when it comes to paying next time your customers are feeling good

- Make the process of paying easy by not making current parents have to fill in another enrolment form

- Respond very quickly to people who want to enroll

- Give a 10% discount to siblings of a child who is enrolled

- Personally thank each parent for re-enrolling and welcome them back

Becoming Profitable

In the beginning of any business there will be more money going out than there is coming in and there will be setup costs to get the business kick started. If you run a dance studio already and you are simply 'adding' the preschool arm to your existing school, you will already have a lot of the infrastructure in place. If you are starting your preschool dance studio from scratch your initial outlay will be higher because you are building everything from the very beginning.

Set Up Costs

A lot of people forget about the starting costs. There is no way of getting around this, the business will not form from thin air, there has to be a budget that is set that you know you can afford. You may have saved the money, borrowed from a family member or secured a personal loan. This kind of business is at a major advantage regarding set up, as it is so low risk. The set up costs may include things like:

- Website set up

- Graphic design

- Props

- Tutus

- Insurances/workers comp/APRA license

- Printing business cards/flyers/Pull-Up Banners

- Facebook marketing/advertising

- Newspaper Advertising

- Postage/stationery

Low Risk/Low Overheads

- No long-term leases – premises can initially be school halls and scout halls on weekly or term rentals.

- No wages going out – in the early days it can be yourself doing all the work.

- No stock – apart from a few props worth only a few hundred dollars, there is no stock that has to be accounted for or insured.

- No expensive websites – a business of this type can have a small, modest website.

Basic Profit & Loss (P/L)

A fair few teachers I speak to do not know their P/L statement. I think it's important to have a good idea of what your weekly P/L looks like. Even if it's rough numbers floating around in your head, that is better than having no idea at all. You can easily get a word document up and use this below as an example of how to get an idea of your incomings and outgoings per week. This allows you to see what you're spending money on.

The great thing about this type of business is that when your student numbers increase a lot of your overhead costs stay the same, so you really are well in front and turning a good profit.

EXAMPLE PROFIT & LOSS

WEEKLY SNAPSHOT (AVERAGE AT 85 STUDENTS AT $16 per class)

TOTAL WEEKLY REVENUE		$1,360.00

Less	Expenses	
	Venues	$182.50
	Insurance/APRA	$19.00
	Marketing (Facebook & Flyers)	$60.00
	Postage	$30.00
	Props (replacement)	$10.00
	Electricity/Phone	$20.00
	Merchant/Bank Fees	$10.00
	Petrol	$20.00
	Miscellaneous	$30.00
Less	**Total Expenses**	**$381.50**

Gross Profit (BOS)	**$978.50**

BOS = Before Owners Salary

The Gross Profit of $978.50 is the funds that can either be paid to the owner-operator or to contracted teachers.

CASHFLOW

It's important to be aware of how much cash flow you have within the business. Focus on the number of students you have and the amount they bring in each week. Any other product sales like tutus, t-shirts or booklets etc are just 'cream' profit, so mainly focus on the actual student fees as your cash flow.

EXAMPLE WEEKLY SNAPSHOT (AVERAGE NUMBERS)

Income Approximate

X LOCATION

Current number of students enrolled for Term 1: 40 students

$16 per student x 40 = $640.00

Y LOCATION

Current number of students enrolled for Term 1: 45 students

$16 per student x 45 = $720.00

Total students based on past average: 85 students

TOTAL INCOME = $1,360.00

In Summary...

- Perceived value is what people pay for.

- Aim your sights on a premium model.

- Focus on your current student retention then focus on new students

- Know your basic 'Profit and Loss'

- Have a 'start-up' budget

CHAPTER 7

THE BUSINESS SYSTEMS

THERE IS SO MUCH TO ORGANIZE CREATIVELY FOR THE RUNNING of the dance side of your studio. You need to plan, organize and arrange an enormous amount of things throughout the year so the studio accomplishes everything you want creatively. Depending on the size of your studio you may have everything from open days, exams, eisteddfods and competitions to summer holiday programs and workshops, showcases and Christmas concerts! All of these things take time, energy and effort not to mention money.

As well as the dance side of the studio there is also the business side of the studio, which includes everything from marketing, invoices and administration to enrolments, accounting and commercial leasing. As the studio director you are project managing both the creative dance side and the strategic business side of your studio.

The more systemized the whole school is, not just certain elements but the school at large – both the dance commitments side and the business side, the more 'on top of it', 'in control' and 'in the drivers seat' you will feel.

Imagine if you had to sell your studio or someone else had to step in for you because of illness or family commitments, you want to create systems that are so tight the person stepping in would be able to pick up where you left off! The best way to think of how to organize your systems is to imagine you have created your own franchise. Franchise systems, models, manuals, policies and procedures not only work for when you have to step aside but for when you're running the studio and want the least amount of hassles. Systems organized with franchise model precision mean that you know what to do when, how to do it and why you're doing it! Systems are set up for everything that needs to be done to achieve the outcomes you want. It's very liberating to have the sensation that your business effectively works on autopilot no matter who's running it.

If you have not picked up the groundbreaking bestseller 'The E Myth' by Michael Gerber I encourage you to do so now. It delves into the reason behind why and how to have great systems in your business.

Here is a quick brainstorm of all the systems we need to have organized in order to run a streamlined school. Depending on the size of your school you may have many more.

- The Marketing System
- The Enrollment System
- The Payment System

- The Customer Service System
- The Teachers & Training System

You may think of others to add to the list. Once you know how to set up a good system there will be no looking back. You may decide to use any number of online systems to also help you organize the backend of your business like Asana, Trello, WAVE APP, Basecamp, Dance Biz, Jack Rabbit or any other system that helps with accounting, team projects and invoices.

The systems I'm mainly referring to are the practical things you need to do in the business on a day to day, week to week, month by month basis. The actual practical stuff you find yourself doing often is the stuff that someone else can easily do if all the 'i's are dotted and 't's crossed within the business.

How to organize:

Work out which system you're going to start creating first. Start with the name of the system on a word doc or whiteboard e.g. Marketing

Brainstorm ALL of the sections of this topic that needs to be systemized planned and recorded.

Under each section of the list you've brainstormed, write down everything you need to do, calendar dates when these things need to be prepared, the flow and order of how things need to be arranged, the contact person etc

For each system we are going to put together a manual. All the manuals for how you operate your business will sit alongside each other in your office – how's that for organization! Anyone who works for you and is designated certain tasks just needs to look at the manual and it will be there! It's a great resource for you as well. When I was running my school I would constantly refer back to my own manuals, as I certainly couldn't remember everything or hold that amount of information in my head.

EXAMPLE

The Marketing System

Brainstorm: (there will be more topics that you can add over time, this brainstorm can become your table of contents in the manual for easy accessibility)

Example of Brainstorm:

- Facebook updates and adverts
- Newspaper submissions and adverts, dance lift outs, editorials
- E-Newsletter to parents
- Annual Fetes
- Dance Shops – cards & communication
- Eisteddfods and competitions – entry dates, costs,

Facebook Updates, Adverts & Spend

EXAMPLE

FACEBOOK STRATEGIC PLAN: What To Put Up On Facebook For Exposure & Engagement

DAY	WHAT TO WRITE
MONDAY	'Ballet Motivation Monday!' Inform your studio of any news, or updates for this week.
TUESDAY	List the location where classes are on and what week it is
WEDNESDAY	Mid week quote and pics of classes
THURSDAY	List the location where classes are on and what week it is
FRIDAY	'Friday Fun' A fun preschooler image or quote
SATURDAY	Saturday class info/location and what's happening
SUNDAY	Only post on special occasions/holidays

You can schedule all this on the Monday so you don't have to think about your updates the whole week. You might do a variety of these updates, you might list your locations and classes everyday or only on days that you run classes.

Your updates can also include:

• Free Trial classes coming up

- Competitions/photos
- Ballet parties
- Images from Demonstration Day
- Preschoolers practicing at home
- Ballet performances coming to your town

Newspaper Submissions and Adverts, Dance lift outs, Editorials

- Write down the names of all the papers in your area
- Write the name/number/website/contact email
- Deadline dates
- Prices for different sizes
- Editorial opportunities

Put all these details into a quick 'go-to' guide either in excel, a folder or another online tool that stores information easily. This becomes a quick tool to look through so you know who and when to submit adverts and stories to. Ensure you then plot every deadline date onto a calendar so you are on track with your marketing and advertising for the year.

E-Newsletters to Parents

EXAMPLE

As mentioned in the marketing module of this 7 Step system – the e-newsletter interaction with parents is really crucial. This gives a very professional impression, it's also fantastic for 'reminder marketing' and staying 'top of mind' and it allows you to advertise to them gently every few weeks.

ENEWS	DATE TO EMAIL	OFFERS/ COMPS	REMINDERS
TERM 1	January 10th	Early bird enrollment	New dance style
TERM 1	WK 1 of Term	NIL	Fees
TERM 1	WK 4 of Term	Mid-term enrollment	Demo Day Dates
TERM 1	WK 8 of Term	Photo comp	Term 2 enrollment
TERM 1	WK 10 of Term	Photos from DDay	Term 2 enrollment

Annual Fete Demonstration

You may have come across some fetes that attract a lot of parents and preschoolers, you may have an opportunity to perform or display at a fete without having to pay a stall-holders fee. If you can arrange a 'deal' with the organizers of the fete, this could be fantastic for you!

List Building

The more you can get seen and noticed in the community the better! Also, remember the number one thing to do when you're at a fete or similar event is to make sure you get the details (name, number, email) of anyone who comes to chat and shows interest in you. This way you can be in touch with them soon about classes. Make sure you ask their permission to be popped onto your e-newsletter list or contacted by phone.

Location, Location, Location for Fetes

My experience of being involved with fetes and festivals is that it will be most effective for you when you participate in a fete which is located in the exact same suburb, town or village where you run the classes. Fetes tend to attract locals from that exact location, meaning, they will generally live in that suburb and wander to the fete after sport, breakfast or shopping. Being local they are interested in products, services and activities that are local.

People don't want to travel. For example if the fete is in Suburb A and your classes are actually operating in Suburb B – I wouldn't advise taking part in that particular fete. Even though it's only a 15-minute drive, people are not inclined to travel very far at all for children's activities. Bottom line - participate in a fete in the exact suburb of your classes or studio if you want it to be as effective as possible.

EXAMPLE

Fetes in Studio Location

FETE	DATE	APPLICATION	COST	OFFER/ DEAL/OPP
Castle Hill Fair	Oct 20th	August 20th	$150	Conduct mini class
Christmas Fair	Dec 20th	June 20th	$250	Christmas show

Dance Shop Communication

People who are successful are good at connecting and communicating with the right people. Businesses that are a match with your industry are people with the same target market as you but not in competition with you. Like you, their customers are parents of dance students.

The good thing about running a preschool focused school is that there are not as many people running pre-school classes only – therefore you do stand out compared to the dozens of schools that offer all sorts of classes for all sorts of ages.

The key is to keep up the communication and contact with dance shops, this will then allow you to display your brochures, pin up your posters and even gain other discounts or offers because you have built up the relationship.

EXAMPLE

Relationship Building at Dance Shops

DANCE SHOPS	CONTACT	CONNECT	THE OUTCOME
Tip & Tap	Darcy Bussell	Feb 5th	Display timetable
Plié Boutique	Moira Sheara	Feb 10th	Display brochures

These tables and lists give you a good idea of the types of systems you need to be incorporating when setting up your dance school or creating a new section of your studio. The best way to organize the manuals is to either hole-punch the sheets and file them into a ring-binder folder or to have them printed and spiral bound at your local stationery store.

The best tactic is to work out what you seem to do more than once, then document it, the rule is – more than once it needs a system!

Another key part of systems is to have a thought out business plan. This can be a 1year, 3year or 5 year plan. It doesn't need to be very long or complicated but it is a useful tool to identify key aspects of your school and your goals and objectives for the school moving forward.

EXAMPLE

Business Plan

Business Idea/Plan/Projection

'Creating a colorful, caring and creative environment for toddlers to learn the expressive skill of dance and movement through uniquely designed programs.'

TABLE OF CONTENTS

Passion/Vision
BHAG/Future goals
SWOT Analysis
Risk Analysis
Budget/Financial Projections – Income Strategy and Outgoings
Competitors in the space
Market Research
Teacher Profile – the job description/profile of the teachers wanted

MISSION (CREATE MISSION)

"At ABC Ballet your child's imagination, creativity and holistic wellbeing is enhanced through our innovative, inspiring and enriching teaching, programs and overall early learning development. We are in the business of creating happy, positive and proactive children who will grow up to live strong, healthy and imaginative lives. We aim to create a colorful, caring and nurturing environment which will impact on each and every one of the children that come to learn with us."

What I want to do/create as a business

I want to create a business which is low on staff, high on cash flow, a target market that is constantly replenished and built around repeat custom. This business also has a system and a format that is completely replicable and most of all it is a positive, passionate and important business that contributes to society and enhances the lives of children.

What is the business?

The business is a dance/movement/drama-based program of classes for the 'tiny tots' age group – 3 – 5 year olds only. The classes are 45 minutes long and operate predominantly 6 mornings per week from 9am – 12 Noon.

Children

My passion is to enhance the lives of young children by providing them their weekly dose of creativity and imagination through exciting programs with engaging dance teachers. The types of words that describe this vision for children is:

Imagination	Creativity	Positivity	Laughter
Inspiration	Individuality	Self-Expression	Color
Learning	Fitness	Friendships	Joy
Focus	Kinesthetic abilities	Motor-skills development	FUN

Teachers

My passion is to also provide strong incomes for women who may need part-time work or Mums who need to work around her family commitments. These types of words describe my passion for women to work in this area:

- Empowerment
- Enhancing the lives of children
- Creating a positive impact on children
- Being an enthusiastic and passionate role model
- Having a commitment and focus on creativity and the imagination
- Developing ones own personal development and enriching her life
- Generating a good source of income
- Contributing to her community and her family
- Touching the lives of others and sharing the vision

GOALS

My broad goal for this business is to do the following:

- Create an incredible brand presence – through color, logo, image and name

- Generate a strong message in the market place focused on the vision and passion behind the business – that of development of individuality, creativity and body awareness.

- Create ship-shape systems that are completely replicable

- Create programs that are completely unique to what is currently in the market place

- Recruit dance/movement teachers that are absolutely on brand and will not be replaceable by just 'anyone'. They will be second to none people and in return treated with utmost importance and priority, paid a solid rate and have continued training and input to develop them not only as holistic, premium teachers but people and women as well.

SWOT ANALYSIS

STRENGTHS
- Niche target market clearly defined
- Large target market
- Low set up costs
- Low staff
- Easy to replicate
- No permanent premises
- Social/community minded business
- Cash business
- Low equipment needs & costs
- No reliance on product
- Positive industry in consumers mind

- Focus on fitness & health in the community because of obesity etc
- Fostering education/creativity
- High paying part-time work for women
- Adding jobs to the work force
- Focusing on women in the community

WEAKNESSES

- Franchise model in this market hasn't really been tested
- New player in the market
- Themed ideas haven't been tested
- Reliant on preschoolers wanting to come to classes
- Reliance on hiring external venues
- Unpredictable age group – can 'go off' activities

OPPORTUNITIES

- Potential alliances with other business in the pre-schooler age group eg. Kids parties, kids costumes, childcare centers
- Replicable model/expansion opportunities
- Leveraging opportunities eg. Refreshments, merchandise, other programs, causes/charities, NFP
- Geographical flexibility – allows for ease in opening and closing certain territories without worrying about employee contracts, commercial leases etc
- Product development – books etc
- Media opportunities/Good exposure for children's creativity, learning and education etc
- This type of business allows for patrons/ambassadors/celeb endorsements – great for exposure.

THREATS

- Competitors in the market place

- Parents wanting to reduce spending
- Parents having less kids
- IP protection issues
- Someone using the same franchise model
- Competing activities for that age group in the same area
- Bad press about dance or movement for young children

RISK ANALYSIS

KEY –

H – High risk

M – Medium risk

L - Low risk

RISK OF TEACHERS LEAVING

Good quality people leaving for the following reasons:

1. Better job offer elsewhere – M
2. Higher pay elsewhere – M
3. Pregnancy – M
4. Moving – M
5. Health – L
6. Family changes/problems – L

SOLUTIONS:

1. Offer excellent working environment with excellent management and support. Invest in building quality relationships with staff that rise above the usual. Invest in training and development of teachers.

2. Offer competitive rate of pay. Same or above the standard.

3. Can work while pregnant as it is not physically stressful and is part time. Teachers encouraged to return.

4. Teacher is supported to set up a new school in their area or work for the existing one.

5. In serious situations may organize fundraiser to support the family. Otherwise show compassion and support to family and work out best solution.

6. Teachers will be supported to become empowered and encouraged to seek assistance with problems or work out the best exit solution.

At all times, the development of positive and well-managed relationships with staff is paramount with development of effective communication skills being given a high priority. Clear boundaries will be set in place through the systems set up.

These solutions generate loyalty and respect through creating a workplace that is high quality.

RISK OF COMPETITIORS IN THE MARKET PLACE

Competitors are those already in the marketplace or potential ones that may move into the area.

- Existing competition – M
- Students leave to go to competitor – M
- Competitor has new or different offerings - M
- Competitor is less expensive – M
- Competitor is more resourced to offer superior experiences – M

SOLUTIONS:

1. Competition in the same location can be good and it can mean that dance classes are in demand and popular but it can also alert a potential problem if there are limited numbers of children in the area/location to patronize your school and the competition.

2. Make the business as compelling as possible so that students and parents want to stay.

3. Our offering is unique to us and their offering will be unique to them. Our POD is our particular brand. Customers will be free to choose.

4. Our rates will be competitive but will reflect the quality of the business. Rates are in the slightly higher range to attract a high quality customer.

5. Our focus will be on the teaching quality, the branding and programs, which are unique to us. We will continually update and modernize to follow trends.

RISK OF TARGET MARKET - PRESCHOOLERS – AN UNPREDICTABLE MARKET?

Toddlers between 3-5 years may present the following challenges:

- Student may not want to continue and parent wants refund - M
- Parent/teacher issues – L
- Preschoolers not liking the classes – L
- Injury or accident – M for minor accidents, L for more serious

SOLUTIONS:

- Parents pay per 10-week term. No refunds. If student leaves then that is a place that another student could have. Can have their spot reserved for the following term as a credit. The remaining funds can be transferred to another child who wants to take the place of the student who has left.

- Teachers will be carefully selected for their enthusiasm and people skills first and foremost. Our aim is to have outstanding customer service. If there is a personality clash the parent will be invited to voice their thoughts and opinions to me if it not resolved by the teacher and parent.

- Classes are designed specifically for preschoolers at the correct developmental level. We focus on creating programs that are cutting edge, at the forefront of learning and development in movement and creativity for young children.

- Preschoolers fall over, this is natural. Teachers will be given health and safety instructions to check. Teachers have to have their own insurance. The venue will be insured. Main aspects to address: flooring quality, footwear. If parents have any concerns regarding anything at all they are encouraged to stay on the premises. Parents will sign terms and conditions forms at the beginning of term covering their responsibility and dance class risk.

RISK OF SECOND TARGET MARKET – PARENT ISSUES

- Thinking the teacher is not good enough or giving their child enough attention – L
- Not liking the programs – L
- Thinking classes are too expensive – L
- Thinking they are not getting value for money – L
- Not liking the outfits – L
- Concern their child is not fitting in – L
- Not liking the time slots – L
- Not liking venue – M

SOLUTIONS:

- Teacher or assistant will have parent's details if there are any emergency issues.
- All parents to be surveyed at end of each year for feedback and changes will be made accordingly.
- We aim to continue to add value with offers and information. We aim to offer same or better value than competitors.
- Outfit will be designed according to feedback from surveys, our brand and age appropriateness.
- Teachers will be trained to be sensitive to different children's personalities.
- There is a wide range of time slots available. Surveys will indicate preferred or disliked days and times. Adjust accordingly.

Income Strategy

Design your own more thorough income strategy based on your current circumstances.

INCOME GROSS FROM TAKINGS APPROX

Class price per week	No of students per class	TOTAL PC
$		$
No of classes per week	No of students per week	TOTAL PW
		$
No of classes per year	No of students per year	TOTAL PY
		$
Merchandise	Purchases	TOTAL PY
		$
	TOTAL GROSS INCOME $	

OUTGOINGS PROJECTION FOR ONE VENUE APPROX

Teacher	Wage per class	Wage per week	Wage per year
Teacher 1	$	$	$
Assistant	**Wage per class**	**Wage per week**	**Wage per year**
Assistant 1	$	$	$
Venue Hire	**Payment per hour**	**Payment per week**	**Payment per year**
	$	$	$
Misc.		**Approx. cost per week**	**Approx. cost per year**
Insurance		$	$
TAX		$	$
Website		$	$
Marketing		$	$
Phone		$	$
Travel		$	$
Stock		$	$
Unaccounted costs		$	$
TOTAL outgoing costs per week			$
TOTAL outgoing costs per year			$

TEACHER PROFILE – JOB DESCRIPTION – IDEAL PERSON

This business is based on professional, ethical, enthusiastic, sensitive teachers who have a passion for children's development and well-being, a love of dance and a commitment to the development of creativity.

I want teachers who understand dance, movement and creativity and ALSO love and understand children and their development.

IDEAL CANDIDATE PROFILE:

- Lives: within 10kms of the venue.
- Qualifications: Must have at least Certificate IV or ideally Diploma or above in any of the following – Dance, Fitness, Yoga, Pilates, Alexander Technique or Physical Culture.
- Experience: Needs to have 3 – 5 years of dance experience.

PERSONALITY/DISPOSITION:

- Energetic, smiling, positive, enthusiastic, happy, upbeat, sensitive, caring, respectful and patient.
- The teachers have a direct impact on the students and need to exude positivity and care. They need to be passionate about what they are doing.

SOCIAL/COMMUNITY ASPECT:

Ideally this person is very social and can get along with all types of people, has a broad network in the community. Ideally involved in local community groups, schools, church etc and loves to be involved in the local community. This community aspect is necessary to build their classes but also to develop effective relationships so that the school becomes positively connected in the community.

LIFE LONG LEARNING:

This person will have a desire and a commitment to continuous learning and development, be open to new ideas, read relevant material and be happy to apply new learnings.

PRESENTATION/ATTIRE

This person takes pride in their presentation and appearance and has high standards of personal hygiene and presentation.

The standard of presentation of the teacher reflects on their commitment to their work and on the way the school is run and on their attitude to their work and their students.

This person will be expected to maintain high standards of personal presentation at all times.

KEY CHARACTERISTICS:

PERSONAL

- Caring, kind and patient
- Nurturing and encouraging
- Gentle yet firm
- Motivating
- Fun, smiley and upbeat
- Thankful and grateful

PROFESSIONAL

- Extremely punctual
- Consistent personality
- Extremely well presented
- Honest
- Highly ethical
- Excellent communication skills

- Excellent customer service skills
- Disciplined and principled
- Respectful and well mannered at all times
- Assertive and grounded

In Summary...

- Have systems for all aspects of the business

- Have these systems written up in manuals for easy access

- Check in to your systems and processes regularly to ensure you're organized and on track and in line with your timeline

- Create a business plan to have clarity around your ideas and projections

- Ensure to include a SWOT analysis in your plan if you're entering a new area or attempting something new in the business

FINAL THOUGHTS

In Review

The synthesis of all these 7 Steps creates a professional, sophisticated and well-run dance studio. It really is the combination of all these steps working together that will have you, your brand and your classes flowing seamlessly. This combination is essential to the effectiveness of your school and the excellence that you can achieve.

In Gratitude

Thank you so much for taking the opportunity and the time to read my book to further yourself to success!

I look forward to possibly working with you in the future, I'd love to hear how your school is going and what you have created – please feel free to email me at: emma@emmafranklinbell.com join my newsletter at www.emmafranklinbell.com or watch my videos on YouTube.

If you want to work with me 1-to-1 to implement the modules in this book, there is some information on the next page.

Thank You

Emma

50% Discount on Private Mentoring

Exclusively for people who
have bought this book!

Take the opportunity to work with Emma exclusively on your dance studio. She will get to the nuts and bolts of how your studio and you personally can be more effective and productive at building a more successful preschool dance studio by following the 7 steps featured in this book!

The Exclusive 90 DAY 1:1 Private Mentoring Program

Delivery:
- 7 x 75min private power mentoring sessions
- Post work set after each session
- Weekly personal accountability check in email
- Unlimited email access 5 days per week
- Plans/Templates and Productivity Tools
- Books you must read
- Investment: ~~$6,499.00 + GST~~

Book today by email to emma@emmafranklinbell.com and quote 'BOOK' and work exclusively with Emma Franklin Bell for your special offer of AUD $3,499.00.

Book Emma Franklin Bell to Speak at Your Next Dance Event.

Are you a teacher, event organizer, editor or industry body executive? Why not take the opportunity to book Emma to speak at your next event. In a keynote presentation, workshop or seminar Emma can dissect, debunk and deliver a presentation based on all or just one of these 7 Steps and have your audience excited, entranced and enthused to take their dance studios to the next level!

Presentation Includes:

Delivery can be:

- 45 minute keynote
- Q & A Session
- Panel Participant
- Workshop 1 – 3hrs
- Seminar 2hrs

Book today or discuss your needs by email: emma@emmafranklinbell.com

About the Author

Emma Franklin Bell hails from a small regional suburb on the Central Coast of NSW, Australia. For 25 years she's been involved in the performing arts industry, primarily dance. She's been involved with dance studios, choreography, performance training, musical theatre, presenting training, theatre sports and street theatre. She has also been a private mentor, reviewer, adjudicator and assessor, curriculum writer, program developer and interviewer on panels for shows, teaching faculties and performance troupes.

Emma has a wealth of knowledge across the areas of business, marketing, performing arts and personal and professional development. Emma has worked for, in and with small businesses for 11 years. Emma's insights and understanding of how to get a small business to work comes from practical application, professional qualifications, a strong skill set and personal first-hand experience.

In 2012 Emma wrote her own preschool ballet program and created, set up and built a ballet school from scratch called Fairy Footsteps. Within 3 months the school had a second location and second teacher with more classes expanding as time went on. Fairy Footsteps was featured in the media and went on to be sold. Emma was administering this business on the other side of the country in Sydney while it operated in Perth. The school still continues to grow several months on and has expanded further.

Emma holds a Bachelor of Communication, Diploma of Business, Diploma of Presentation Skills, and a Certificate of Dance Teaching (QUT). Emma is a caring and thoughtful woman who has walked many paths and her passion is to add value to other people's lives to inspire, develop and take them to a higher level. She believes everyone has the resources within them to live their best life and wake up with purpose and passion.

Lightning Source UK Ltd.
Milton Keynes UK
UKOW01f1824030916

282119UK00002B/76/P